A Practical Guide to Quantum Computing and the Law

A Practical Guide to Quantum Computing and the Law

Laura Wright

Barrister, 4 Pump Court

Called England & Wales (2014)

Rebecca Keating

Barrister, 4 Pump Court

Called England & Wales (2017), Republic of Ireland (2019)

Law Brief Publishing

Published 2024 by Law Brief Publishing, an imprint of Law Brief Publishing Ltd
30 The Parks
Minehead
Somerset
TA24 8BT

www.lawbriefpublishing.com

Paperback: 978-1-916698-60-4

FOREWORD

The law is only just beginning to grapple with the full implications of artificial intelligence: critical issues concerning intellectual property rights and liability remain undecided by the courts; new legislative frameworks emerging across the world are yet to be tested. Yet, as this book reminds us, AI is by no means the final technological frontier to which the law needs to respond and adapt. Development continues apace, not least in the guise of quantum computing, the challenges of which are fast appearing over the horizon.

Quantum computing today perhaps bears more resemblance to a laboratory experiment than a revolution in practical computing. However, as Wright and Keating warn in this fascinating book, the legal implications and risks of this nascent technology are already beginning to arise. That is in part because, with substantial activity and investment flowing into the sector, technology lawyers are already having to draft contracts that cater for liabilities flowing from quantum computing and that reflect the intellectual property landscape in which quantum computers reside.

Perhaps the biggest issue identified in the book, however, is the impact of quantum computing on cryptography and, in particular, the risk that access to quantum computing will allow threat actors to break with ease the cryptographic algorithms on which most modern security depends. Wright and Keating acknowledge ongoing work to develop and implement quantum-secure replacement algorithms, but they also point out that new-generation algorithms are far from a panacea in a world where threat actors are *already* exfiltrating and storing large volumes of encrypted information with the aim of decrypting them at a later date once sufficient quantum computing resources is available. This cryptography threat, together with the fact that it is already a *known* threat, gives rise to the possibility that statutory liability under data protection legislation or common law liability in tort may in future arise from quantum computing as a result of steps taken or not taken by custodians of data *today*.

Thus, even though Wright and Keating are writing at a time when there is very little substantive law squarely dealing with quantum computing, *A Practical Guide to Quantum Computing and the Law* is a timely book that technology lawyers should read.

Matthew Lavy KC
4 Pump Court
23rd October 2024

PREFACE

Quantum computing is set to revolutionise important aspects of the way we live and work. While it may feel to some readers to be in the realms of science fiction, significant advances have been made in quantum computing in the last decade and will continue to gather pace in the coming years. As quantum computing continues to develop, we felt there was a need for a book that not only explores legal issues that are on the horizon, but also the legal issues occurring in practice today. This book therefore aims to address both current and future legal issues in order to assist lawyers as the adoption of quantum computing becomes more widespread.

In addition to exploring the legal issues that arise as a result of the increased use of quantum computing, we hope readers will also gain an insight into the exciting developments that quantum computers will bring.

The technology and law described in this book are accurate as of 30th September 2024. However, both of these areas are subject to rapid change.

Laura Wright
Rebecca Keating
October 2024

ACKNOWLEDGEMENTS

Laura would like to thank her parents for their unwavering support. However, she would like to make it clear that just because she has written a book about quantum computing, that does not mean she knows what has gone wrong with their printer/email account/online banking.

Rebecca would like to thank John, Miriam, Ruth, Matthew and Alex for their support and listening to her seemingly unending chatter about the multiverse.

CONTENTS

CHAPTER ONE

INTRODUCTION

From the advent of the internet to the widespread use of artificial intelligence, technology can, and has brought, significant changes in the ways we live and work. Quantum computing is no exception.

The nature of law is that it often focuses on risks and so, naturally, legal textbooks can appear overly focused on the downsides of new technologies. This book may appear no different. We write about a range of legal issues that may arise from privacy issues, national security frameworks and IP issues. However, we hope readers will also catch a glimpse of the possibilities that quantum computers will facilitate. There is much to be excited about.

Estimates of how long it will take to have access to quantum computers which have 'quantum advantage', a term explored later in the book, vary between five and thirty years from now. However, it would be wrong to think, as lawyers, that legal questions are not already arising. For example, there are already legal issues in respect of the acquisition or export of quantum computers, IP considerations such as obtaining patents for quantum computing hardware and software, and significant cyber security issues. As the use of quantum computers become more prolific, legal issues will increase.

Quantum computing is a developing and complicated area. This book attempts to distil the key aspects of quantum computing so that lawyers are aware of some of the legal issues arising out of the adoption and use of quantum computing. In attempting to distil the issues, at various points we have simplified the underlying technology or processes involved. For those interested in understanding the technology in greater detail, the authors cite various resources in the footnotes which are worth exploring in greater detail.

CHAPTER TWO

WHAT IS QUANTUM COMPUTING?

Terminology

Before delving into the intricacies of quantum computing, we must first address a matter pertaining to the nomenclature utilised in this text. At various points, by way of comparison, we will refer to a "classical computer", meaning the computers that we are familiar with and use day to day (which includes supercomputers). These are distinct from quantum computers. You may find when you read more widely on the topic of quantum computers various terms are used to refer to a classical computer – digital, conventional and even analogue. There is much discussion over the appropriate term to use. Some argue that "digital computers" are a misnomer, given the computers we use day to day have not worked in standard digital form since the 1940s as modern computers use binary rather than decimal form. Strictly speaking "quantum" is the opposite of "analogue" but in the context of quantum computing it refers to specifically to computers which harness the power of quantum particles. In this book, we assign no significance to the use of the term classical computer, save to denote the kind of machines with which we are all familiar.

This book focuses on quantum computers specifically.[1] In various pieces of legislation, which we will explore in greater detail later in this

1 ISO/International Electrotechnical Commission C 4879:2024 (the "**ISO/IEC 2024 Standard**") has developed a standard specifically for terminology and vocabulary for quantum computing. Edition 1 was

book, "quantum technologies" are referred to. Quantum technology is a much broader term which does not yet have a universally accepted meaning.[2] Quantum computing is a branch of quantum technology. Quantum technology more broadly refers to a field of engineering and computer science which harnesses the power of quantum mechanics but results in a broader range of technologies than just computers, for example creating quantum batteries or sensors. Therefore, while quantum technology encompasses quantum computing, the terms should not be used interchangeably.

What is a quantum computer?

A classical computer is a device that, by virtue of being dependent on electronics (which focuses on the behaviour of electrons), is dependent on quantum physics. However, largely they do not harness the power of quantum particles in the way that quantum computers do.[3]

On the other hand, a quantum computer harnesses the special properties of quantum particles in order to perform certain operations. As a result of those special properties, it is possible to not only perform

---

published in 2024. The document defines terms commonly used in the field of quantum computing. The objective of the document is that it can be applicable to all types of organisations (e.g. commercial enterprises, government agencies, not-for-profit organisations) to exchange quantum computing concepts. Readers may find this a useful resource if drafting agreements relating to quantum computers. We return to this point later in the section dealing with risks to commercial parties and organisations.

2 The IEEE have a working group which is developing standard terminology for quantum technologies more generally (IEEE P7130).

3 Save in respect of arguably the use of quantum tunnelling in flash memory storage.

computational calculations faster than a classical computer, but also to carry out tasks that would not be possible with a classical computer.

This history of quantum computing, how a quantum computer is built and how they might work in practice, is addressed in greater detail below. It is worth noting at the outset that the below is intended to give a sense of how quantum computers may be designed and operate, in order to grasp a little of how they differ from classical computers. This is done at a high-level not only because as lawyers we are not trying to design quantum computers ourselves, but more importantly because the rate of development is quick. What is intended to be current as at the time of writing, will likely be different in the months and certainly years that follow.

Therefore, we hope the following discussion gives an insight into the differences between classical and quantum computers and, by virtue of how they are designed and may operate, the legal issues which arise in respect of quantum computers that may differ from classical computers.

Short history

We live in a quantum world. Quantum physics and quantum mechanics shed a light on our understanding of how our world operates. Quantum theory or quantum mechanics developed in part for scientists to be able to account for some physical phenomena that were inherently uncertain. This context is an important backdrop to the development of quantum computers.

In 1981 Professor Richard Feynman gave a keynote at MIT.[4] Feynman suggested that a computer could be built to simulate the probabilistic nature of quantum interactions which would make it a more realistic model for quantum behaviour. Classical computers struggle in simulating quantum behaviour partly because of the difficulty in reproducing randomness. Feynman's lecture therefore proved an important point in the development of quantum computing.

Fast forward to 2018 onwards and many companies are competing for what is known as quantum supremacy or quantum advantage. We return to this concept later in this chapter.

Therefore, in understanding what quantum computers are, and how they work, it is important to remember that quantum computers were conceived of, at least initially, as a way to understand quantum physics itself. This is therefore relevant to considering not only how they work but how users can utilise these computers and their capabilities.

Benefits

Before addressing how a quantum computer may be built, we address at a high level what the benefits are. The practical significance and use cases of quantum computers are explored in greater detail later in this next chapter of this book.

It is worth noting the limits on the exponential growth possible with classical computers. Those familiar with Moore's Law will know it states that the number of transistors that can fit on a silicon chip doubles every two years. Quite simply, there are limits on the

4 Feynman, R.P. Simulating physics with computers. Intern. J. Theoretical Physics 21, 6/7 (1981).

exponential improvement possible with classical computers. Therefore, it is worth keeping in mind as we address the benefits of quantum computers, this general context that there is a limit on how much classical computers will ever be able to develop and improve.

At a high level there are two key advantages to quantum computers. The first, is the ability to carry out a computational task far quicker than a classical computer and the second is the ability to perform tasks that are beyond the capability of a classical computer. The line between the two can, on occasion, be hard to distinguish i.e. can a quantum computer perform a task because: (i) it is able to perform a task exponentially faster (i.e. making intractable problems tractable); or (ii) because quantum computers are actually performing the task in a different way.

It would be a mistake to believe that quantum computers can perform a task that classical computers cannot merely because they are faster. That is not the case. Quantum computers can also perform tasks that classical computers cannot by virtue of the fact they harness the power of quantum particles and therefore are better suited to certain tasks. It is not the case with comparing a computer that merely has greater computational power by virtue of enhanced speed. We address each benefit in turn below.

Turning to the first key benefit – speed. For certain problems, digital computers are unable to give a useful answer in a realistic time scale because the number of possibilities to assess are too great. However, quantum computers can represent multiple states at once and therefore provide answers in a realistic and useful timeframe in response to those questions.

There is of course a drawback to speed, which many readers will be aware of, which is the impact on internet security. This point is explored in greater detail in Chapter Five, which covers security breaches and data protection.

The second key benefit is solving problems that are beyond the reach of classical computers. Simulations are one example where quantum computers offer the potential for significant advances. For example, the European Patent Office commented in its decision in *Pedestrian Simulation* [2021] E.P.O.R. 30, which relating to the patentability of computer-implemented simulation of pedestrian flows in architectural designs, at paragraph 115 that "*[s]imulations may even require computer power which is not available from a standard computer (for example, quantum computing could be necessary for turbulence or molecular simulations).*" It is worth adding that it is not just a question of computational power but also the distinct way in which quantum computers approach simulations of, for example, molecules, which make them better suited to these tasks. For example, classical computers cannot accurately calculate how atoms combine to create important chemical reactions. Robert Sutor, vice president of IBM, often makes the following comparison: for a classical computer to re-create a one-to-one simulation of a simple molecule, like caffeine, it would require 10^{48} bits of information. To put that figure in context, that represents 10% of the number of atoms making up planet earth.

Hence, classical computers cannot successfully simulate even simple molecules. Classical computers often rely on approximations to simulate complex systems like atoms. While a single hydrogen atom can be solved relatively easily, adding more electrons, like in helium, makes the calculations exponentially more complex. Quantum computers, like Google's Sycamore, have shown promise in simulating these systems more accurately, as demonstrated by its simulation of a

12-atom hydrogen chain.[5] At scale, it is anticipated that fully operational quantum computers could be 100 million times faster than today's classical computers and even taking supercomputers, at least 3,500 times more powerful.[6]

The use cases are wide including in pharmaceuticals (addressed in Chapter Three on the practical significance of quantum computers below) where simulating complex biological and chemical processes. For example, trying to model the penicillin molecule with a classical computer would take 10^{86} bits of computer memory. This is beyond the capability of a classical computer but within the capability of a quantum computer.

Finally, it is worth noting that quantum computers are not intended to replace classical computers. They are not being designed to have that effect. The first point is that classical computers are relatively robust machines that execute well the tasks we require. Even turning to specialist functionality, quantum computers will most likely require classical computers to support their specialised abilities and so classical computers, even in the dominion of the quantum computer will remain important and relevant. For example, a research group at IBM is collaborating with bankers JPMorgan Chase & Co.[7] The objective

---

5 See 'Google has performed the biggest quantum chemistry simulation ever' published in New Scientist on 12 December 2019 available at https://www.newscientist.com/article/2227244-google-has-performed-the-biggest-quantum-chemistry-simulation-ever/.

6 Page 7 of Jeffery Atik and Valentin Jeutner (2021): "Quantum computing and computational law, Law, Innovation and Technology" available at https://doi.org/10.1080/17579961.2021.1977216.

7 See '11 Global Banks Probing The Wonderful World of Quantum Technologies' in Quantum Insider (23 June 2021) available at https://thequantuminsider.com/2021/06/23/11-global-banks-probing-the-wonderful-world-of-quantum-technologies/.

is to develop a quantum algorithm in order to accelerate pricing options. While it utilises quantum computing, it is based on IBM's cloud-based computing service. It is therefore a combination of classical and quantum computing.

Furthermore, IBM Quantum Platform (previously known as IBM Q Experience) is a publicly available service whereby users can access quantum computers via a cloud-based service.[8] Readers of this book may be interested in trying out the IBM Quantum Platform to browse tutorials but also to run experiments and explore use cases. However, again the pertinent point is that this indicates at least in the near to middle future access may be via the cloud for quantum computing where the quantum computer itself is located in a specialist environment (with appropriate cooling and vibration controls).

Qubits and building a quantum computer

John Preskill asked two key questions in 1998: [1] do we want to build quantum computers and [2] can we build them?[9] This section deals with that second question. There is not a universal method of building a quantum computer. However, from the point of view of lawyers, what this section seeks to achieve is an understanding of the basic building blocks and methods that are being explored to answer Preskill's second question.

Fundamental unit – quantum/bit

Bits in classical computers are binary in nature in that they are represented by either a "0" or a "1" ("*classic bits*"). Classic bits are

---

8 The IBM Quantum Platform is available at https://quantum.ibm.com/.

9 John Preskill, 'Quantum Computing: Pro and Con' (1998) 454 Proceedings of the Royal Society of London A 469, 469.

therefore open or closed and are a traditional logic gate. Each bit is a small circuit. These circuits are typically comprised of one or more transistors and a capacitor (a component that holds an electrical charge which represents 1, or no charge which represents 0).

Quantum computers are constructed using a basic unit of operation which is not limited in the way that classic bits are. A quantum bit, known as a qubit,[10] is based on a quantum particle for example an electron or photon. Typically it is measured in terms of spin or polarisation. In contrast to classic bits, a qubit is not binary, it can be a 0 or 1 (as with a classical computer) but can also be any linear combination of the two (superposition). It is therefore in an intermediate state with a potentially infinite set of possibilities of which state it is in. This is a fundamental and crucial difference between a classical and quantum computer.

The practical significance of this difference is that a quantum computer can conceive of more than one result at any particular moment in time. Three conventional bits can store any one number between 0 and 7 (binary 000 to 111). However, three qubits can make use of all eight numbers simultaneously. A binary string of eight bits, also called a byte, can represent any of 256 possible values. We will return to the number of possible values that classic bits can hold versus quantum bits in the context of superposition.

While currently quantum computers are largely used as effectively a compute unit for classical computers, it is possible to programme a quantum computer and therefore utilise the unique logic gates that go beyond the capability of a classical computer.

Those familiar with the workings of classical computers will wonder what coding language a quantum computer uses. In short, in classical

---

10 A portmanteau of quantum and bit.

computers, source code is run through a compiler (a program which converts source code into assembly language). The result is then run through another program which generates executable code. In quantum computers no standardised program has emerged. It may be that given quantum computers can be neatly represented by matrices that there may be resurgence in a variant of APL, as some commentators in the industry have speculated, but this is yet to be seen.

Quantum theory

At a high level, the theory behind quantum computers is that storing information in a superposition of states and manipulating their value (using quantum interactions such as entanglement) allows for new types of algorithms.

Understanding the theory behind how quantum computers work is difficult and in itself merits a book, indeed many books. As a lawyer, it is not necessary in order to explore the issues below to understand the theory behind quantum computers in granular detail. However, there are a number of key concepts which are useful to understand, even at a high level, in order to understand why quantum computers are different to classical computers and accordingly, the distinct legal issues that stem from them.

There are a number of key concepts that underpin how quantum computers work and how they differ from classical computers, these are [1] superposition, [2] entanglement, [3] sum over paths and [4] tunnelling. The first two are particularly important and therefore are addressed in greater detail below.

Superposition

A key element of classical computers is that they analyse information in a binary way using either ones or zeros. This is a fundamental difference to the way that quantum computers operate and is crucial in understanding the potential power of a quantum computer.

In a quantum computer the range of possibilities for the state of a qubit is greater before it is measured. When the quantum spin of a particle is measured, it only be either "up" or "down". However, the before the particle is measured, it is in a superposition of states – it is therefore both up and down at the same time. Therefore, only probabilities exist.

Many readers will be familiar with Schrodinger's Cat and therefore the idea, at a very high level, that it is not possible to know the state of something (in that case a cat) until a measurement is made. Perhaps an easier way to conceptualise superposition is to imagine a spinning coin; before the coin is observed and a measurement made, all that exists are possibilities as to what state the coin is in.

Logic gates operate in a different way in quantum computers versus classical computers. Classical computers have circuits that as act as logical gates performing a function such as NOT or AND. Quantum gates are more complex, as they operate on multiple possibilities at any one time. However, quantum gates can perform many calculations at once and, unlike classic logic gates (apart from NOT), quantum gates are reversible.

Entanglement

Entanglement is an important part of connecting a quantum computing system. In short, a change in one particle is instantly reflected in another particle. This occurs even if the particles are separated by large distances. For example, if one particle is measured as spin down, the other particle would instantly become spin up.

Accordingly, each time another qubit is added, it interacts with the previous qubit and so the number of possible interactions doubles. The practical impact is an exponentially powerful computer.

Entanglement improves the processing speed of quantum computers because it allows them to manipulate many qubits in a single operation, instead of manipulating each qubit individually.

It is worth mentioning that entanglement is often misunderstood and often explained incorrectly in articles. It does not allow actual information to be transmitted faster than the speed of light because the results of quantum measurements are random, so it will never be able to overcome the delays involved in contact with deep space missions. For example, if communications are being sent as between Earth and Mars the results will not be instantaneous and will take around twenty minutes depending on the relative positions of Earth and Mars in their orbits.[11]

[11] See https://www.physicsforums.com/threads/mars-landing-how-instantaneous-communication-was-possible.999911/#:~:text=The%20time%20it%20takes%20for,travel%20from%20Earth%20to%20Mars.

Methods of building a quantum computer

In theory any quantum particle could be used. However, in practice simple particles are selected on the basis that they are easier to deal with. For example, photons and electrons as opposed to a water molecule. A few benefits of photons are that they are relatively easy to produce in controlled environments, are plentiful and are the easiest to get into an entangled state. Electrons are also a good choice as we are familiar with electrons (given our knowledge of electronics). However, each have their drawbacks in practice. Larger quantum particles have also been used including ions. IonQ system makes using of ytterbium ions.[12]

In terms of specific methods based on the above:[13]

- Superconducting quantum computers. An example is Sycamore, which is discussed in the section below in the context of the race for quantum supremacy. The advantage is that they use silicon as a base, which has been used in industry for decades. By cooling circuits to near absolute zero, they enter a quantum state where electrons can exist in multiple states simultaneously. When these circuits are connected, they can become entangled, enabling quantum calculations. A major drawback of this method is the complex system of tubes and pumps required to cool the machine to extremely low temperatures. This increases costs and introduces potential complications. Even the slightest disturbance or impurity can disrupt the coherence of the circuits. One solution is to use

---

12 See IonQ's website for further details https://ionq.com/technology.

13 For a more detailed discussion of the various methods of building a quantum computer "Quantum Supremacy" by Michio Kaku (2023).

multiple qubits to create redundancy and reduce errors, but this comes at the expense of significantly higher costs.

- Ion Trap Quantum Computer. When an electrically neutral atom loses electrons, it becomes a positively charged ion. Ions can be trapped using electric and magnetic fields, and multiple ions can vibrate coherently as qubits. The spin of the electron determines the qubit state (0 or 1), allowing for superposition. However, scaling up the number of qubits is challenging, as maintaining coherence requires constant readjustment of electric and magnetic fields, making it a complex process.

- Photonic Quantum Computers. Photonic quantum computers use light's polarisation to represent 0 and 1. While they offer advantages like speed and the ability to operate at room temperature, their complex setup and difficulty in interacting photons limit their scalability and practicality.

- D-Wave Computers. D-Wave, a Canadian company, is developing quantum annealing, a specialised type of quantum computing. D-Wave has built machines with up to 5,600 qubits and plans to increase this to 7,000 in the near future, surpassing other current designs.[14] Though they are not general purpose quantum computers, they can solve certain problems very quickly.

The inner workings of these methods are beyond the scope of this book save to note that the relevance for lawyers is that there is not a universal method for building a quantum computer. There are advantages and disadvantages to each of these methods and therefore

---

14 See https://www.hpcwire.com/2024/06/18/qubits-2024-d-waves-steady-march-to-quantum-success/.

the risks and benefits regarding each needs to be evaluated depending on the technology used.

Quantum algorithms

With a classical computer the hardware is often considered first. However, with quantum computing, quantum algorithms have existed well before quantum computers were able to, or indeed can, run these algorithms. It has proved possible to devise algorithms for quantum computers which, should a reliably functioning quantum computer be built, could revolutionise the world of computing. The patentability of quantum algorithms is discussed in the chapter dealing with quantum computers and intellectual property below.

A few examples are explored in this book to give a flavour of the type of use cases that will arise in practice. For example, an algorithm known as Grover's quantum search algorithm makes it possible to carry out "fuzzy" searching (a genuine technical term).[15] In terms of the practical application, while search engines operate at generally impressive speeds, they rely on inputting relatively precise search terms in order to reach the desired result. However, this is different to the usual pattern making that most humans use day to day.

Taking an example, if the authors wanted to locate the address of a "*red brick building in London with flower boxes, black boards with barristers' names to the right and left of a white framed door. The building*

---

15 Acampora, Giovanni & Luongo, Federico & Vitiello, Autilia. (2018). Quantum Implementation of Fuzzy Systems through Grover's Algorithm. 1-8. 10.1109/FUZZ-IEEE.2018.8491579. For further reading on Grover's underlying work see Grover, L. K. Quantum mechanics helps in searching for a needle in a haystack. "Physical Review Letters79", 2 (1997) and Grover, L. K. A fast quantum mechanical algorithm for database search. In "Proceedings of the 28 Annual ACM Symp." Theory of Computing, 1996. ACM, New York, NY, 212–219.

itself is located in a courtyard which is adjacent to the lane where Mary Poppins Returns was filmed" this would not yield the result 4 Pump Court in a Google search. However, this is the kind of pattern matching our brains are used to. It is also the kind of fuzzy searching which Grover's algorithm handles well. It completes a search using just the square root of the number of operations of a classical search, thus speeding up the ability to provide a useful result exponentially faster than a conventional computer. This would have practical applications not just for search engines but also quantum machine learning.

Shor's algorithm is another example of a quantum algorithm which is discussed in more detail in the chapter on the practical significance of quantum computing and in the chapter on security breaches and data protection.

Challenges of building a stable quantum computer

Building a stable quantum computer is one of the greatest practical challenges facing those designing quantum computer systems. There are two core issues [1] ensuring qubits stay in a stable state and [2] transferring information in and out of the computer.

One of the major issues in building a stable, and therefore useful, quantum computer is reducing the risk of errors or incorrect information. If you take expressing the probability of weather with a classical computer, weather forecasting is difficult because the underling system being studied (weather) is chaotic in terms of the calculations that take place due to shifting variable terms. Quantum computers are vulnerable to errors given the components are so sensitive and thus qubits can lose their quantum state. As a result, quantum computers can store or manipulate information incorrectly. The errors then accumulate over time. This in turn prevents them from executing algorithms (which are based on the premise of stable qubits unaffected by their environment) that are long enough to be of use. A system of error elimination or correction is therefore needed.

In order for a quantum computer to function reliably, the qubits need to remain in phase with each other but isolated from their surroundings (called coherence). Decoherence is used to refer to the effect where quantum particles, through their interaction with their environment (such as vibrations or temperature) lose their superposed state. Qubits are very sensitive and so even a minor disturbance can cause them to fall out of coherence and so render the calculation unreliable. For superconducting qubits the 'coherence time' is typically only around a millisecond.

The computing industry is familiar with the need for specialist environments. Think for example of a traditional server farm. Therefore, similar consideration needs to be given to rectifying errors in quantum computers.

Google Quantum AI, along with its academic collaborators, have conducted research which was released in August 2024 which shows that adding components can reduce errors. The experiments were conducted using qubits based on superconducting circuits.[16] As noted above, previously adding more components tended to introduce more errors. However, this research indicates that error correction, as opposed to elimination, is viable method of building a reliable, and therefore useful, quantum computer.

In short, many methods of designing quantum computers have focussed on each unit of information being stored in a single physical qubit. However, Google's research has focused on encoding each unit of information in multiple physical qubits. This group of multiple

16 MIT Technology Review, "The Download: quantum breakthrough, and the Internet Archive ruling" (September 2024).

qubits is referred to as a single "logical" qubit. The benefit is that this logical qubit can hold information in a more robust form than a single physical qubit. Google's research team then used an algorithm known as a surface code to correct errors. However, the number of qubits is large. Google demonstrated that a logical qubit composed of 105 physical qubits suppressed errors more effectively than a logical qubit composed of 72 qubits. However, Google and its researchers are yet to demonstrate they can scale up to a larger machine.

By way of another example, IBM (also using qubits made of superconducting circuits) is taking a different approach to error correction known as low-density parity-check code. It believes this will be easier to scale (as each qubit requires fewer physical qubits). By 2026, IBM plans on proving that it can create a system that uses 12 logical qubits out of 244 physical qubits.[17]

The key point to appreciate regarding error correction, from the vantage point of a lawyer, is that [1] quantum computers are, at least in their current form, susceptible to errors and [2] there needs to be a system for eliminating or correcting errors which is relevant to assessing the reliability of a quantum computer. For example, as explored in greater detail below, if two parties are contracting for the use of a quantum computer it will be relevant to consider what level of errors is acceptable and what degree of reliability one can expect from the quantum computer system.

17 See "Google enhances quantum error correction technology" by Adam Campbell featured in Baseline (September 2024).

Race for quantum supremacy or quantum advantage

The race for quantum supremacy and quantum advantage brings out some of the achievements, but also the limitations, of quantum computing, both at present and perhaps into the future.[18]

In September 2019 Google announced that its quantum computer, Sycamore, had achieved "quantum supremacy".[19] In short, quantum supremacy is the short-hand term used to describe a quantum computer outperforming a classical computer. While a significant development, other technology companies competing in this area did note, somewhat fairly, the introspective nature of the task assigned to Sycamore. In simplified terms, Sycamore was tasked in proving whether the numbers it had generated as random were in fact random. Google stated this task would have taken the world's fastest supercomputer 10,000 years. In 2020, the Quantum Innovation Institute at the Chinese Academy of Sciences stated that their quantum computer was 100 trillion times faster than an ordinary supercomputer.[20]

One way to view these announcements is that they do mark exciting developments in quantum computing. Other technology companies

---

18 The term 'quantum practicality' is also used. For a wider discussion on the terms used and the search to realise quantum advantage "Disentangling Hype from Practicality: On Realistically Achieving Quantum Advantage" by Hoefler, Häner and Troyer (available at https://cacm.acm.org/research/disentangling-hype-from-practicality-on-realistically-achieving-quantum-advantage/) is a useful resource.

19 See https://www.nasa.gov/technology/computing/google-and-nasa-achieve-quantum-supremacy/. The project was run in partnership with NASA and Oak Ridge National Laboratory.

20 See https://www.tbsnews.net/tech/chinese-scientists-claim-have-built-quantam-computer-100-trillion-times-faster-japans-fugaku.

state they are aiming for quantum advantage whereby quantum computers outperform in respect of useful, rather than theoretical tasks. Setting aside the terminology, estimates vary between five and thirty years for when we may see quantum advantage being attained.[21]

It is not just private companies that are investing time and money in reaching quantum advantage. In December 2018, the US Congress passed the National Quantum Initiative Act.[22] Part of that initiative was to provide seed money to assist in research. In the UK, in July 2024 five hubs for the National Quantum Computing Centre ("**NQCC**") were announced.[23] The NQCC focuses on research and innovation. They also engage with industry and researchers in drafting documents and surveys relating to quantum readiness. At a European

---

21 See https://www.insidequantumtechnology.com/news-archive/quantum-cryptographic-threat-timeline. In 2023 the UK Government published its long-term quantum missions following the commitments made in its national quantum strategy policy paper, which it published in March 2023. There are five missions relating to quantum computing. While not necessarily an accurate reflection of what progress will be achieved, it is useful to note that the missions list 2030 and 2035 as the year by which the UK aims to have achieved its stated missions relating to quantum computing including by 2035 there will be accessible, UK-based quantum computers capable of running 1 trillion operations and supporting applications that provide benefits well in excess of classical supercomputers across key sectors of the economy and the UK will have deployed the world's most advanced quantum network at scale, pioneering the future quantum internet.

22 Public Law No: 115-368 (12/21/2018) available at https://www.congress.gov/bill/115th-congress/house-bill/6227#:~:text=Shown%20Here%3A-,Public%20Law%20No%3A%20115%2D368,(12%2F21%2F2018)&text=(Sec.,information%20science%20and%20technology%20applications..

23 See https://www.ukri.org/news/five-hubs-launched-to-ensure-the-uk-benefits-from-quantum-future/.

level, the EU has invested heavily in quantum technology, launching initiatives like the Quantum Flagship and developing the European Quantum Communication Infrastructure.[24] These programs aim to advance quantum research and create a secure quantum communication network across all EU Member States.

Ethical considerations

There are a variety of important and engaging debates regarding ethical concerns surrounding quantum computers. These range from privacy concerns (stemming from, for example, the potential security risk posed by quantum computers), to concerns regarding national security (linked with the security risk) and environmental concerns (given certain designs for quantum computers require, for example, energy intensive cooling systems).

These issues are addressed throughout this book to the degree they are relevant to considering legal issues which practitioners may face in practice. However, this book does not purport to opine on the veracity or otherwise of these concerns or the balance to be struck between these competing concerns. Should readers be interested in exploring these issues further the various sources cited in the footnotes of this book explore those issues in greater detail.

---

24 See https://digital-strategy.ec.europa.eu/en/policies/european-quantum-communication-infrastructure-euroqci. In 2018, the EU also created the EuroHPC Joint Undertaking to enable the EU to become a world leader in supercomputing and quantum computing, by pooling the resources of participating EU countries and private partners. On 13 July 2021, the Council Regulation (EU) 2021/1173 established the European High Performance Computing Joint Undertaking and repealed Regulation (EU) 2018/1488.

Summary

In the preceding paragraphs we have discussed what a quantum computer is through the lens of history, the ways these machines work (or may work) in practice and the race for quantum advantage. As noted in the introduction, this is an area subject to significant change and development. However, the basic principles set out above should serve as both a useful guide to readers in the present, and in the future in exploring the legal issues that arise in respect of quantum computing. Before embarking on that discussion, we explore in a little more detail the practical significance of quantum computing as a way of providing a useful framework for considering the impact these computers will have on individuals and various industries.

CHAPTER THREE

THE PRACTICAL SIGNIFICANCE OF QUANTUM COMPUTERS

Introduction

As set out in the preceding sections, the use of superposition and entanglement will, in time, enable quantum computers to [1] identify causal relationships and solve problems faster and more efficiently than classical computers and [2] solve new problems. However, the widespread use of quantum computers is still some years away. The quantum computers currently in operation can perform basic quantum operations, but their computational power is still small compared to classical computers. In April 2024 the management consulting firm McKinsey predicted that progress in quantum computing would remain slow, with a fully fault-tolerant quantum computer not being expected until 2035 at the earliest.[25] The following advancements still need to be achieved:

- Hardware development: There is no definitive hardware for quantum computers. Quantum companies such as IBM, Google, IonQ and PsiQuantum are each experimenting with different technologies, such as superconducting qubits, trapped ions, and photonic systems (discussed above in Chapter Two).

---

25 See https://www.mckinsey.com/featured-insights/mckinsey-explainers/what-is-quantum-computing.

- Scalability: While significant technological milestones have been achieved (for example, and as referred to in Chapter Two above) in 2019 Google achieved what they termed quantum supremacy (meaning their quantum computer solved a problem faster than the fastest classical computer), quantum computers have yet to be scaled up in practice. In order to have practical, real-world applications, quantum computers will need to have a much larger number of qubits.

- Error correction: As noted in Chapter Two above, a key area of research has been error correction for quantum computers. Like all computers, quantum computers are prone to errors. Correcting those errors is complex due to the fact that each qubit exists in a mixed state of 0 and 1. Error rates in quantum computers have, to date, been too high for practical use. At the time of writing, Google Quantum AI has just announced the building of a quantum computer that makes fewer errors as it is scaled up. This could pave the way for machines that solve real-world problems for the first time.[26]

In order to overcome these challenges, there will need to be sustained investment in quantum research and development by the public and private sectors. As briefly discussed above, there has been a lot of investment at a national and international level into quantum computing. The UK has, in the past decade, made significant investments in quantum technologies:

- The National Quantum Technologies Programme was a ten-year project launched in 2014 which was aimed at developing

26 See https://www.newscientist.com/article/2446071-google-breakthrough-paves-way-for-large-scale-quantum-computers/.

quantum computing in the UK.[27] The programme established four quantum technology hubs.

- The UK National Quantum Strategy was launched in March 2023 under Rishi Sunak's government.[28] It was designed to continue the work of the National Quantum Technologies Programme, the strategy set various goals to be achieved by 2033 and promised a further £2.5 billion of government funding. The objectives of the strategy include funding research and supporting skills development in quantum technologies, helping UK companies to bring quantum innovations to market, supporting businesses across different sectors in their adoption of quantum technologies, and focussing on national security in the age of quantum computers.

- A key component of the UK National Quantum Strategy is the NQCC, discussed in Chapter Two above. Based at the Harwell Science and Innovation Campus in Oxfordshire, the NQCC has been funded by the public body UK Research and Innovation and is expected to be fully operational by 2025.

Whilst the above projects have been established and some of them funded, future investment in quantum computing is not a certainty. In August 2024, the UK Government decided to withdraw £1.3 billion of investment in technology and AI projects more broadly.[29] The Department for Science, Innovation and Technology explained that while funding had been promised by the Conservative

---

27 See https://uknqt.ukri.org/our-programme/.

28 See https://www.gov.uk/government/publications/national-quantum-strategy.

29 See https://www.bbc.co.uk/news/articles/cyx5x44vnyeo.

government, it had not been allocated in spending plans. Journalists have suggested that these cuts could leave the UK reliant on other countries for access to the latest quantum computing developments. An article published in The Times in September 2024 described how founders of Phasecraft, a UK-based quantum computing startup, had warned that the withdrawal of funding had unnerved the industry and that concerns are growing over Britain's ability to compete with the United States and China.[30] Phasecraft expressed their concerns in a paper and called for sustained and consistent public investment, international collaboration, and responsible regulation.[31]

The following sections explore how, if investment into and development of quantum computing continues apace and technological advancements are made in the next few decades, quantum computing may:

- Be used in conjunction with AI and machine learning;
- Impact different industries;
- Accelerate research in important fields; and
- Impact classical computers, and in particular the effect of quantum computing on the encryption that protects classical computers.

30 "UK risks being left behind in quantum computing", Richard Tyler, The Times, 10 September 2024.

31 See https://www.phasecraft.io/news/future-of-qc-white-paper.

The Impact of Quantum Computing on AI and Machine Learning

As discussed above, certain limitations of classical computers will be overcome by quantum computers. Quantum computing's integration into artificial intelligence ("**AI**") and machine learning ("**ML**") (sometimes known collectively as Quantum AI, or "**QAI**") is an emerging field. The use of the enhanced computational capabilities of quantum computers, as well as new quantum algorithms, will lead to improved accuracy of predictions, and better pattern recognition. QAI will be of particular significance to AI and ML research in the following ways:

- Speeding up model training: Quantum computers can perform multiple calculations simultaneously, meaning that they can process large amounts of data much more quickly than classical computers. This will reduce the time required to train machine learning models.

- Solving optimisation problems: Prevalent in machine learning, optimisation problems involve finding the best solution from all possible solutions. Solving these problems will be transformed by the use of quantum algorithms such as the Quantum Approximate Optimisation Algorithm ("**QAOA**"). The QAOA uses a sequence of quantum gates to encode the optimisation problem, and iteratively searches for a solution.

- Enhanced data processing and feature selection: Quantum computers can analyse multi-dimensional datasets more effectively than classical computers. Machine learning, at the pre-processing stage, involves feature selection and extraction. Put simply, the number of input variables used in a model is reduced by removing irrelevant or redundant features, thereby improving the quality of a model's classification. Further, Quantum Principal Component Analysis ("**qPCA**") is a dimension reduction technique which can process large datasets exponentially faster than the equivalent on a classical computer, meaning that the data underlying ML models can be simplified more efficiently and the model's performance improved.[32]

There are already examples of the combination of quantum computing and AI; in 2022 the quantum hardware and software quantum company IonQ partnered with Hyundai Motor Company. The two companies have been working on quantum powered chemistry simulations in order to improve the durability and safety of lithium batteries (a form of quantum technology),[33] as well as quantum machine vision algorithms capable of conducting object detection on three-dimensional data from autonomous vehicles.[34]

---

32 See https://doi.org/10.1016/j.physleta.2019.06.026.

33 See https://www.hyundai.news/eu/articles/press-releases/ionq-and-hyundai-partner-to-use-quantum-computing-to-advance-effectiveness-of-next-gen-batteries.html.

34 See https://ionq.com/news/ionq-and-hyundai-motor-company-expand-quantum-computing-partnership.

The Impact of Quantum Computing on Industry and Areas of Research

Quantum computing could revolutionise a wide range of industries and research areas.[35] The following sections briefly explore how the increased computational power and problem-solving capabilities of quantum computers could be employed in:

- The financial services sector;
- The chemical and pharmaceutical industries;
- Business operations; and
- Energy and environmental research.

Banking and Financial Services Sector

Quantum computing has the potential to significantly transform the financial services industry by offering unprecedented computational power and efficiency for complex tasks. Classical computers do not have the resources to solve the large and complex optimisation problems that face financial institutions, whereas quantum computers could make portfolio management and trading more efficient. Similarly, the use of quantum powered machine learning and AI could result in faster training and implementation of models, leading to more accurate market predictions. Finally, quantum computers will

---

35 While not an area we have focussed on in this book, it is possible that the legal sector would also benefit from the power of quantum computers. For more information see Page 7 of Jeffery Atik and Valentin Jeutner (2021): "Quantum computing and computational law, Law, Innovation and Technology" available at https://doi.org/10.1080/17579961.2021.1977216.

be able to simulate large financial systems and model financial markets, thereby providing insights into market trends.

In a report jointly authored in November 2023 by IBM and the trade association UK Finance, risk analysis was identified as one of a number of key opportunities presented by quantum computing.[36] Quantum computing could enhance the modelling of financial risks by simulating complex market scenarios more accurately, thereby allowing for earlier identification of risk, the precise estimation of risk metrics, and improving the ability to manage financial exposures. Quantum computers could also be used by financial institutions and regulators to predict customer behaviour.

The other opportunities identified in the UK Finance report include:

- Compliance: Quantum computers could lead to the automation and optimisation (by quickly identifying patterns and discrepancies in datasets) of regulatory compliance processes.

- Investments: Portfolio optimisation and asset management could be improved by identifying quickly optimal investments strategies and maximising returns while minimising risks.

- Sales: The use of enhanced data analytics could result in new markets being identified and personalised products offered to customers.

---

36 See 'Seizing the Opportunities: Quantum Technology and Financial Services', https://www.ukfinance.org.uk/system/files/2023-11/Seizing%20the%20opportunities%20-%20quantum%20technology%20and%20financial%20services.pdf.

- Pricing: Complex market data could be analysed quickly and optimal pricing strategies identified in order to ensure competitive pricing.

- Fraud detection: The real-time analysis of large datasets to detect anomalies could result in enhanced fraud detection and better AML checks.

Similarly to the adoption of AI in the financial services and banking sectors, there will in due course likely be industry specific guidance.[37] There have already been some statements issued by the Bank of England[38] and the Financial Conduct Authority.[39] These have not given rise to industry guidance specifically. However, those working

---

37 Ofcom, the ICO, the Bank of England and the Financial Conduct Authority have all issued various reports relating to quantum technologies, including the use of quantum computing.

38 For example, see the Bank of England's 2023 report entitled "The digital pound: Technology Working Paper" available at https://www.bankofengland.co.uk/-/media/boe/files/paper/2023/the-digital-pound-technology-working-paper.pdf.

39 In July 2021 the Financial Conduct Authority published an article regarding the potential of quantum technologies in the financial services sector. Available at https://webarchive.nationalarchives.gov.uk/ukgwa/20240308012256/https://www.fca.org.uk/insight/quantum-leap-financial-service. In January 2024, the Financial Conduct Authority, in collaboration with the World Economic Forum, published a white paper regarding the quantum threat to public-key cryptography and key considerations for transitioning to quantum-secure systems. Available at https://www.weforum.org/publications/quantum-security-for-the-financial-sector-informing-global-regulatory-approaches/. See also the UK Finance report entitled "Minimising the Risks: Quantum Technology and Financial Services" (November 2023) for a wider discussion on the use of quantum computing in financial services.

in financial services and adopting quantum computing should consider if there is any relevant industry guidance which may be published in the coming years. What is clear from the work published by the Financial Conduct Authority and the Bank of England is that quantum computing is set to have a significant impact on the banking and financial services industries both in terms of the adoption of this technology but also there will be an impact by third party use (for example in respect of security).

The Chemical and Pharmaceutical Industries

Quantum computing has the potential to revolutionise chemical and pharmaceutical research.[40] As explored above in Chapter Two, to date it has been impossible for classical computers to undertake molecular simulations to a high degree of accuracy due to an inability to compute the trillions of possible configurations of electrons.

Quantum computers operate using qubits which can represent multiple states simultaneously. This means that quantum computers could be used to simulate larger, more complex molecules, leading to more accurate research into the properties and behaviours of these molecules. The development of molecules is at the heart of pharmaceutical research. Vast amounts of money, as much as 15% of sales in some companies, are spent by pharmaceutical companies on

40 While we focus on the impact on chemical and pharmaceutical industries, there is also huge potential in the field of medicine more broadly. As noted above, in 2023 the UK government set out its long-term quantum missions. It is useful to note that Mission 3 was stated to be that by 2030, "*every NHS Trust will benefit from quantum sensing-enabled solutions, helping those with chronic illness live healthier, longer lives through early diagnosis and treatment*".

research and development.[41] In an effort to curb these costs, the pharmaceutical industry has long been an early adopter of new technologies such as molecular dynamic simulations and AI. Pharmaceutical research could be further accelerated, and effective treatments developed more quickly, by the use of quantum computers to simulate, in a virtual environment and without the need for physical experiments, the interaction between drug molecules and their target proteins. Possible uses of quantum computing in pharmaceutical research include:

- Predicting more accurately how proteins fold and interact with other molecule in order to design drugs which bind more effectively with proteins;

- Using quantum optimisation algorithms to identify the best molecular structure for new drugs;

- Discovering more efficient reaction pathways and discovering new catalysts, thus making pharmaceutical research more energy efficient;

- Modelling DNA and RNA molecules and their interactions with other molecules in order to improve genetic treatments such as CRISPR-based therapies;

- Replacing animal testing and clinical trials with using quantum computers to screen compounds;

41 See https://www.mckinsey.com/industries/life-sciences/our-insights/pharmas-digital-rx-quantum-computing-in-drug-research-and-development.

- Reduction of side-effects by using quantum computers to simulate complex biological processes; and

- Predicting, and reducing, the byproducts created by different chemical reactions so as to reduce waste products in the pharmaceutical and chemical industries.

The UK government has recently invested in the use of quantum technologies to improve healthcare. In June 2024 a partnership was announced between the Cleveland Clinic in the US, the UK's Science and Technology Facilities Council ("**STFC**") Hartree Centre, and IBM, to develop advanced computing applications for healthcare and life sciences.[42] The partnership will receive £210m of funding over five years, and the first projects to be undertaken will focus on the use of AI and quantum computing to improve healthcare globally. Just a month later, in June 2024, the Department for Science, Innovation and Technology announced that £100m in government funding had been promised in order to establish five quantum hubs in universities in Glasgow, Edinburgh, Birmingham, Oxford, and London.[43] These hubs will work on developing practical uses of quantum technology, including quantum computing, to improve medical scanners, blood tests, and new surgical interventions and treatments.

42 See https://assets.publishing.service.gov.uk/media/66a94b00ab418ab05559300e/SIN_US_Impact_Story_Q1_2425.

43 See https://www.gov.uk/government/news/over-100-million-boost-to-quantum-hubs-to-develop-life-saving-blood-tests-and-resilient-security-systems.

Business Operations

Quantum computing is expected to transform how businesses operate, particularly in terms of data processing and optimisation, product development, and supply chains and logistics:

- Data processing and optimisation: As discussed above, quantum computing will allow businesses to process large datasets faster, and to solve optimisation problems. As an example, in 2020 the international courier and delivery company DHL earmarked quantum computing as a key trend, and gave the simultaneous packing of parcels as an operational process that could be expedited by the use of quantum computing.[44]

- Product development: Materials and processes can be simulated using quantum computing in order to test for durability and the complexity of manufacturing. This will lead to more innovative products, and a reduction in the cost and energy usage of manufacturing.

- Supply chains and logistics: Complex logistical problems could be solved by the use of quantum algorithms. Dynamic route optimisation, a process which involves using real-time data choosing the optimal route in order to improve efficiency and reduce cost could result in faster and more sustainable delivery methods.

---

44 See https://lot.dhl.com/quantum-computing-could-transform-the-logistics-industry-within-the-next-decade/.

Energy and Environmental Research

Quantum computers could accelerate research into energy usage and climate change. The following are the key areas in which quantum computing may solve complex problems:

- Climate modelling: Quantum computers increased computational abilities will mean that more precise climate models can be produced. These will allow researchers to predict more accurately the impacts of climate change.

- Optimisation of energy resources: By solving optimisation problems, quantum computers may be able to manage distributed energy resources including grids which integrate different types of power source. Intermittent energy sources such as solar and wind could be managed so as to make these renewable energies more reliable.

- Energy storage: As discussed above in the context of pharmaceuticals, quantum computers can simulate the behaviour of molecules. This could have a significant impact on the development of batteries and fuel cells, leading to more efficient energy storage for use in electric vehicles and renewable energy grids.[45]

- Chemical reaction and catalyst simulation: The ability to simulate complex interactions at a molecular level may also help optimise the production of hydrogen, and the

---

See further "How quantum computing can help tackle global warming" https://www.mckinsey.com/capabilities/mckinsey-digital/our-insights/how-quantum-computing-can-help-tackle-global-warming.

development of new catalysts to make reactions more energy efficient.

- Carbon capture: Quantum computers may be able to, by simulating the chemical reactions involved in trapping carbon dioxide, aid in the design and optimisation of carbon capture and storage technologies.

The Impact of Quantum Computers on Classical Computing

Quantum computers will have a significant impact on classical computers. It is not, however, anticipated that quantum computers will replace classical computers entirely, rather they will be used alongside each other. Quantum computers will likely be employed as specialised tools in areas where their ability to solve complex problems is desirable. Examples of such use across different industries are given in the preceding section. For most other tasks, such as using the internet, classical computers will remain the more cost-effective option.

The parallel use of quantum and classical computers poses some challenges, the most significant of which being that the encryption techniques which protect classical computers are vulnerable to quantum computers.

RSA encryption is one of the most widely used public-key cryptographic systems in the world. Developed in 1977, it was named after its creators Ron Rivest, Adi Shamir, and Leonard Adleman. RSA is used for secure data transmission. It underpins digital signatures, digital certificates, some email encryption, authentication of parties using VPNS, and, importantly, communication protocols such as TLS and SSH. These protocols are used to establish secure connections between web browsers and web servers.

The security of RSA relies on the practical difficulty of factoring the product of two large prime numbers. While not unbreakable, a classical computer would take such a long time to perform this calculation as to not be a practical option to break the encryption. Computer scientists consider it practically impossible for a classical computer to factor numbers longer than 2048 bits, which is the basis of the most commonly used form of RSA encryption.[46]

Quantum computers, however, would be able to crack RSA encryption with ease. Shor's Algorithm, devised in 1994 by mathematician Peter Shor, is a quantum algorithm designed to factor large integers into prime factors. Shor demonstrated that a sufficiently powerful quantum computer could factor numbers longer than 2048 bits with ease, thereby making RSA encryption crackable. Unlike any factoring algorithm run on classical computers, Shor's algorithm runs in polynomial time rather than exponential time, meaning that the time required for the algorithm to execute increases at a manageable rate as the input size increases. It was Shor's Algorithm for factoring large integers that first brought quantum computing to the attention of national governments and industry alike. Shor essentially proved that, in time, quantum computers will be able to break RSA encryption. However, this is most likely still some decades off. Scientists have yet to build a quantum computer powerful enough to run Shor's Algorithm. It has been estimated that a quantum computer would need around 20 million qubits to run the algorithm. At the time of writing, the most power quantum computers have just over 1000 qubits.

In light of the possible impact of Shor's Algorithm on RSA encryption, classical computer systems will likely have to move towards the

46 See https://www.technologyreview.com/2019/05/30/65724/how-a-quantum-computer-could-break-2048-bit-rsa-encryption-in-8-hours/.

widespread use of quantum-resistant encryption algorithms. Research is already being done in the field of "post-quantum cryptography", ("**PQC**"), with cryptographers preparing for the day when current algorithms will be vulnerable to quantum computing attacks. PQC research is mostly focussed on the use of lattice-based, multivariate, hash-based, code based and isogeny-based cryptography, as well as symmetric key quantum resistance. A common feature in these types of cryptography is that they require a larger public key size than those currently used.

The impact of quantum computing on RSA is explored in greater detail below in the sections regarding security breaches and data protection and risks to commercial parties.

CHAPTER FOUR

NATIONAL SECURITY AND SANCTIONS

Introduction

Legislation addressing national security and sanctions are two of the rare areas where lawyers will currently be able to locate specific rules regarding quantum computers.

In the UK transactions involving quantum computers are regulated. The concerns are primarily two-fold, the first relates to national security concerns and this is then coupled with the risk of UK businesses being acquired in hostile takeovers.

As set out above in Chapter Two, quantum technology is a much broader term than quantum computing. The legislation referred to below which addresses quantum computing covers quantum technologies as well. The terms as used in the legislation are referred to as the rules are broader than just those governing quantum computing.

National Security and Investment Act 2021 (Notifiable Acquisition) (Specification of Qualifying Entities) Regulations 2021/1264

The National Security and Investment Act 2021 (the "**NSI Act**") grants the Secretary of State powers to scrutinise and intervene in certain acquisitions of control to safeguard the UK's national security. In addition, the range of transactions is broad and includes not just mergers and acquisitions but also minority investments, acquisitions of voting rights and acquisitions of assets including land and IP. The UK Government has the power to review relevant deals that took place from any point after the date the bill was published (i.e. deals entered into or completing on or after 12 November 2020). However, the full regime applies only from 4 January 2022. Failure to comply may result in turnover-based fines and criminal liability or transactions being declared void.

The NSI Act repealed section 23A of the Enterprise Act 2001 (which previously was relevant to mergers and acquisitions relating to quantum computers). Therefore, to the extent practitioners are involved in advising such acquisitions, the NSI Act is the governing piece of legislation.

Quantum technologies come within the mandatory notification regime. The trigger events for mandatory notification are:

- The acquisition of more than 25 per cent, more than 50 per cent, or 75 per cent or more of the voting rights or shares in a qualifying entity.

- The acquisition of voting rights enabling or preventing the passage of any class of resolution governing the affairs of the qualifying entity.

For the purposes of this book, and deciphering if quantum computers would come within the scope of quantum technologies, it is worth noting that schedule 13 relates to quantum technologies specifically. Quantum technologies are broadly defined at paragraph 2 of schedule 13 of the NSI Act as follows:

"quantum technology" means—

(a) quantum communications;

(b) quantum connectivity;

(c) quantum imaging, sensing, timing or navigation;

(d) quantum information processing, computing or simulation; or

(e) quantum resistant cryptography"

"Quantum information processing, computing or simulation" is later defined as:

"(a) the simulation or realisation of systems that use certain properties of quantum mechanics, specifically superposition or entanglement, to acquire, encode, manipulate or process information, run algorithms or perform operations or measurements on data;

(b) algorithms, applications, software, error correction, noise reduction and operating systems that enable the functionality of the system;

(c) the capability of a classical computer to represent the internal state and operations of a quantum computer ("quantum emulation"); or

(d) the hosting or provision of third-party access of a quantum information processing, computing or simulation cloud-based service"

Accordingly, quantum computing would fall under the definition of "*quantum information processing, computing or simulation*" and also potentially there would be overlap with the other limbs, depending on the functionality involved.

There are certain exceptions which are set out in guidance to the NSI Act:[47]

- An entity undertaking solely fundamental research into quantum information science.
- An entity which uses use quantum goods or services provided by others, without having played a part in developing or producing the technology. For example, an energy company that purchases a quantum sensor to detect emissions of greenhouse gases.
- An entity that supplies a component for use in a quantum technology system, for example a company that provides a dilution refrigerator for use in the development of quantum computing technology.

Therefore, while certain exceptions apply the application is generally very broad.

47 See https://www.gov.uk/government/publications/national-security-and-investment-act-guidance-on-notifiable-acquisitions/national-security-and-investment-act-guidance-on-notifiable-acquisitions#quantum.

Export Control

There has in recent years been an increased focus on emerging technologies including quantum computer technologies and by extension products which incorporate quantum computing technology.

The scope of sanctions is outside the remit of this book, however it is worth noting that quantum computers, for similar reasons they are regulated under the NSI Act, are often expressly referred to in the context of sanctions and export controls.

On 11 March 2024, the UK government issued new amending regulations, the Export Control (Amendment) Regulations 2024. This updated the existing regime comprising of the Export Control Order 2008 and the retained EU Dual-Use Regulation.

The updated rules impose new export controls which relate to quantum technologies. From 1 April 2024 a licence is required for the export of these to any destination. Quantum technologies are, similarly to the legislation discussed above, broadly defined. The controls include quantum computers, qubit devices and qubit circuits, quantum control components and quantum measurement devices and computers.

Similar export control regimes apply in Spain, France and the Netherlands. Therefore, it is part of a broader tightening on export controls relating to quantum computers as governments appreciate the potential impact of these technologies.

Sanctions

Finally, quantum technologies are often referred to in the context of sanctions. Taking the Russian Sanctions and Belarus sanctions, quantum computing falls within the scope of "restricted goods". The 14 April 2022 Russia (Sanctions) (EU Exit) (Amendment) (No 8) Regulations 2022 (SI 2022/452) makes amendments to the Russia (Sanctions) (EU Exit) Regulations 2019 (SI 2019/855) by introducing new trade sanctions measures and amend existing trade sanctions measures for the purposes set out in regulation 4 of the 2019 Regulations. New restrictions are made to trade in relation to a number of goods including quantum computing.

CHAPTER FIVE

SECURITY BREACHES AND DATA PROTECTION

Introduction

One of the more immediate issues that arises in the context of quantum computers is the impact it has on traditional IT security systems and therefore privacy and data protection concerns.

However, it is a quantum paradox of sorts – quantum computers offer the possibility of greater protection but risk exposing vulnerabilities for weaker traditional systems.

Current encryption methods are vulnerable as computational power increases. Quantum computing has the potential to undermine current encryption systems, as addressed in greater detail below. Therefore, current cryptographic algorithms lose their defence against the enhanced computational power that quantum computers possess.

Indeed, the ICO's second Tech Horizons Report 2024 noted that commentators had disclosed to it concerns regarding "*harvest now, decrypt later*" activities.[48] In short, malicious actors are collecting high

[48] The report is available at https://ico.org.uk/media/about-the-ico/research-reports-impact-and-evaluation/research-and-reports/technology-and-innovation/tech-horizons-report-1-0.pdf. In the autumn of 2024 the ICO released an additional report specifically on quantum technologies available at https://ico.org.uk/media/about-the-ico/research-reports-

value information now with a view to decrypting it once the capability of quantum computers becomes available.

Conversely, the development of quantum cryptography will pose enhanced opportunities to protect data, for example the Jinan network in China. The possibilities, as well as the risks, are addressed in greater detail in the following paragraphs.

Risks

Current common encryption methods and Shor's algorithm are discussed above in the section addressing the impact on classical computing. In short, Shor's algorithm could render our current internet security systems redundant. Shor's algorithm sounds relatively benign – the ability for a quantum computer to work out which two prime numbers have been multiplied together to produce an integer. However, current security systems are based on the premise that it practically very difficult to extricate two primes from a multiplication. Therefore it is not that the code is unbreakable so to speak, it is that it is very hard to break given the time required to break the code. These encryption methods typically use variants of an algorithm called RSA (in essence taking two extremely large prime numbers and multiplying them together). For example, even to factorise a 200 digit number would take centuries for a classical computer. This is known as a trapdoor function – multiplying the two numbers is simple, but to reverse the calculation would take a very long time.

impact-and-evaluation/research-and-reports/technology-and-innovation/ico-tech-futures-quantum-technologies-1-0.pdf.

The obvious risk is essentially a brute force attack. Brute force attacks are where a threat actor uses trial and error to access a system (usually through an automated system).

The increased computing power and capabilities of quantum computers therefore poses a risk as regards threats to conventional security, data leaks and loss of information. While such attacks may not be an immediate concern, as noted above, the ICO has commented that some actors are already collecting data on the basis it will be possible to decrypt that data at a later point. Accordingly, the risks are not merely future concerns, but current problems.

Improving protection

There are two possible ways of looking at the issue of how to improve security. The first is to examine how current security systems operate and improve those operations using classical computer methods. The second is to consider how quantum computers may themselves be utilised.

Before turning to quantum encryption, it is worth noting that there is a lot of time and money being invested in developing quantum-proof encryption. For example, instead of continuing the reliance on RSA, Advanced Encryption Standard ("**AES**"), an existing technique is being further developed, which may mean that it would be too hard for a quantum computer to break AES in a sensible time. Quantum-resistant lattice-based systems are also being developed. The significant point for lawyers, in particular those focused on data or privacy, is that traditional methods of security may not be adequate. It is not simply the case that organisations and individuals may wish to explore methods of quantum encryption but also quantum-proof methods, which rely on classical computers.

In terms of harnessing the power of quantum computers, by virtue of the properties of entangled particles these represent a naturally random set of values. As long as the particles stay entangled, the encryption is not breakable.

Data protection and privacy

Reduced security capabilities tie in with data protection and privacy rights. As noted above, the proliferation of quantum computers will make the risk of private or confidential information being exposed a greater concern. However, data is being harvested at present on the basis that one day it will be possible to decrypt it. Therefore, it is important for lawyers to analyse the risk not only the basis of what issues may arise once quantum computers are more prolific but also how data is currently protected, as it may be at risk of being collected now and decrypted at a later stage. While there may be an argument to be made about what are reasonable systems to have in place to protect against a quantum computer, if data is susceptible to harvesting by a classical computer, companies and organisations may still be subject to the criticism, and accordingly liability, in that they have not adequately discharged their duties to protect data adequately.

Companies and organisations will need to keep under review the developing concept of an obligation to protect against a quantum threat. While at present that may appear to be a remote concern, if in due course data is decrypted using quantum computers, what systems an organisation or company had in place to protect data from unlawful access will be relevant. There will then be the question of how that data was protected from decryption.

The NQCC (in collaboration with EY),[49] the US National Institute of Standards and Technology ("**NIST**") and the European Telecommunications Standards Institute ("**ETSI**") have issued guidance documents to assist organisations in considering quantum readiness. All institutions acknowledge that the real threats are still some years away. However, these organisations also encourage industry to consider and prepare for the impact of quantum computing on security.

The NIST recommend that one way organisations can prepare for the increased security threat, if the organisation is reliant on RSA, is to increase the number that has to be factorised. It may be in due course that quantum computers will be able to break even this modified or enhanced RSA, but it may delay access (certainly those currently harvesting information for later decryption) and in the future still make it prohibitively expensive for a quantum computer to break. However, the most direct way to address the issue is for more sophisticated encryption methods to be adopted, which are more complex than the original RSA code. The NIST addresses several of these new algorithms. In August 2024 NIST finalised its principal set of encryption algorithms designed to withstand cyberattacks from a quantum computer.[50] However, in practical terms these algorithms can be difficult to implement, so whether they are capable of being adopted and also stop or reduce a quantum threat, remains to be seen.

---

49 See https://www.ey.com/content/dam/ey-unified-site/ey-com/en-uk/insights/emerging-technologies/documents/ey-quantum-readiness-survey-2022.pdf.

50 See https://www.federalregister.gov/documents/2024/08/14/2024-17956/announcing-issuance-of-federal-information-processing-standards-fips-fips-203-module-lattice-based.

In 2022 the US brought in the Quantum Computing Cybersecurity Preparedness Act[51] which aims to address the potential threat of quantum computing to current encryption protocols used by the US federal government. The act mandates several actions:

- Inventory and Prioritisation: Agencies must inventory vulnerable information technology systems and prioritize them for migration to post-quantum cryptography.

- Migration Planning: Within a year of NIST issuing post-quantum cryptography standards, agencies must develop migration plans.

- Reporting to Congress: The Office of Management and Budget must submit a report to Congress detailing the strategy to address vulnerabilities, funding needs, and progress on NIST standards.

Overall, the Act seeks to ensure that federal agencies are prepared for the potential impact of quantum computing on cybersecurity. It is a useful international example of specific legislation aimed at dealing with the impact of quantum computing on security.

Governments and large organisations may have the means to adopt quantum cryptography, as opposed to adopting enhanced classical computer methods. For example, in the future governments may use a separate internet channel based on lasers, as opposed to electrical cables. As laser beams are polarised, it would be immediately apparent if a message was intercepted. Accordingly, it may be that governments or banks may use this enhanced form of the internet in the future. Quantum key distribution ("**QKD**") is another form of new technology being explored. In short, entangled qubits mean it is

51 See https://www.congress.gov/bill/117th-congress/house-bill/7535/text.

possible to detect if a third party is hacking into a network. Toshiba has predicted that QKD may generate up to $3 billion in revenue by the end of this decade.[52]

In due course organisations and companies may face claims similar to those that currently arise where a company or organisation has been the victim of a data breach. It is not adequate to argue that the company or organisation's data has been unlawfully accessed, perhaps even as a result of criminal activity.

In terms of the existing legal framework regarding data protection, under the Data Protection Act 2018 and UK GDPR,[53] organisations have an obligation to:

- Ensure the confidentiality, security and integrity of the personal information they process.

- Take appropriate technical and organisational measures to protect this information.

A few points that may be relevant for considering liability:

- Did the organisation adequately (either by reference for example to data protection or contractual standards depending on the nature of the claim) protect data against harvesting or collection by reference to current cryptography standards?

52 See https://www.reuters.com/article/technology/toshiba-targets-3-billion-revenue-in-quantum-cryptography-by-2030-idUSKBN2730KV/.

53 Readers should also have regard to the broader privacy framework including the Privacy and Electronic Communications Regulations and the Regulation of Investigatory Powers Act 2000.

- What relevant industry guidance was available regarding quantum threat?
- What steps could the organisation reasonably have taken to guard against quantum threat?[54]

Accordingly, the authors consider that organisations and businesses will need to consider reevaluating and reenforcing their security measures, to protect against both the current risks of harvesting of data for future decryption, and also attacks facilitated by the increased computational power of quantum computers.

Impact on blockchain and smart contracts

The impact of quantum computing on blockchain networks is again premised on the impact of quantum computing on cyber security. Take for example, a cryptocurrency, which is a decentralised system which is often premised on trust achieved through cryptographic methods. Accordingly, if those cryptographic methods become less effective or even obsolete, this has an impact on the blockchain network.

Deloitte has estimated in its "Quantum Cyber Readiness" report that as of July 2022, 25% of Bitcoin and 66% of Ether are vulnerable to quantum threat.[55] In terms of when Deloitte estimates this threat will

---

54 It may also be relevant to assess whether the organisation undertook a data protection impact assessment in adopting new quantum computing methods such as QKD.

55 See https://www2.deloitte.com/content/dam/Deloitte/us/Documents/risk/us-risk-deloitte-quantum-cyber-readiness-perspective-2022.pdf.

materialise, it was set out in the report as sometime after 2030 but before 2035.

Criminal activity

For the same reasons that quantum computers will impact on data protection and privacy, quantum computers may also be relevant in the context of law enforcement and new criminal behaviour. On 23 October 2023, Europol published a new report looking at the impact of quantum computing and quantum technologies on law enforcement. The report was drafted by Europol's Innovation Lab in cooperation with the European Commission's Joint Research Centre and Europol's European Cybercrime Centre.[56]

Summary

One of the most significant impacts of quantum computers being used alongside classical computing is the impact on security. As explored above, there are enhancements to current classical computing methods of cryptography being developed, as well as methods of using quantum computing itself to protect personal data and confidential information. It would be wrong to assume this is an issue that is only on the horizon. As addressed above, concerns are already arising regarding harvest now, decrypt later processes. Therefore, companies and organisations should be considering not only how they will be quantum ready in the future but also how they can discharge their

56 See https://www.europol.europa.eu/cms/sites/default/files/documents/Europol_Innovation_Lab_Observatory_Report%20-%20The%20Second%20Quantum%20Revolution.pdf.

current legal obligations to protect data in order to guard against decryption in the future.

CHAPTER SIX

RISKS TO COMMERCIAL PARTIES AND ORGANISATIONS

Introduction

At the outset it is worth noting that while there will be disputes that require a specialist knowledge of how quantum computers work, there will of course be disputes relating to quantum computers and the provision of such services which are ordinary disputes and commercial matters that arise in the context of any industry. For example, in the US the case of *BV Advisory Partners, LLC v Quantum Computing Inc.*, C.A. No. 2022-0719-SG. The case involved a dispute arising from a merger between Quantum Computing Inc. and QPhoton. The Plaintiff alleged that the merger undervalued QPhoton and that certain defendants breached their fiduciary duties. The case itself however is an example of what one might call a "traditional" piece of litigation, where the underlying technology itself is largely irrelevant to the key issues in dispute.

Therefore, the following paragraphs focus on specific issues where the underlying technology may be relevant to the legal advice sought or the dispute that arises.

Security risk

As set out above, there are security concerns that arise in light of the increased computational power of quantum computers. Accordingly, organisations and companies will need to assess and evaluate their current and future IT systems to ensure they are complying with their obligations under data protection, privacy rights and other obligations regarding protecting confidential information.

The two points of that lawyers should consider in particular are:

- Developing guidance from bodies such as the ICO regarding what standards are expected of organisations and companies in light of this risk.
- In contracting for IT services and insurance contracts, considering whether systems meet the required standards to guard against attack and unlawful access and who is responsible in the event that a security incident takes place.

Contracting for quantum computers

The points set out above largely focus on the inadvertent impacts of quantum computers on companies and organisations, as opposed to parties who are actively contracting for quantum computers.

National security, sanctions and export controls

As set out above in Chapter Four there are specific points that arise regarding the acquisition of quantum computing businesses or assets. There is therefore specific legislation that applies in those types of scenarios.

Contracting for quantum computing systems

As set out above, there are a variety of use cases for quantum computers across different industries including banking and financial services, medicine and pharmaceuticals. Industries that are data intensive in particular will benefit from quantum computers.

There are a number of points which parties should consider when contracting for the use of quantum computers:[57]

- Parties will need to take particular care in selecting the definitions used in agreements which relate to quantum computers. Lawyers may find it useful to have regard to the ISO/IEC 2024 Standard, referred to in the footnotes of the terminology section above, as a starting point in considering what may be suitable definitions to adopt in the agreement between parties.

- Parties will need to consider what constitutes a reliable result? As set out above, quantum computers [1] express results as a matter of probabilities and [2] can be, depending on their design, more prone to errors. In any event, if contracting for quantum computing services, it will be important to consider what is a reliable result or what constitutes the system performing to the required standard. Not only will parties need to consider this from a commercial perspective, in order to consider the utility a system offers, but in the event that parties consider that a system is underperforming, how will the parties evaluate performance.

---

57 It is worth noting that linked with the potential impact on cyber security, there is a risk that digital signatures could become an issue where third parties forge signatures to impersonate the legitimate private key owner or alter information where the authenticity is protected by a digital signature. Given this is not a specific concern regarding contracting for quantum computers it is not addressed in the list of points to consider when contracting for quantum computing but is another point that lawyers should be aware of when considering the validity and authenticity of documents and how they may be protected in the future.

- Parties will also need to have regard to practical considerations regarding access to quantum computers. It may be that access is generally via a cloud-based system.

- Parties will need to carefully examine liability provisions. Parties are well aware of the significance of considering limitation and exclusion of liability provisions. However, in the context of quantum computers parties will need to consider whether traditional wording and limitations adequately address the parties' needs.

ESG considerations

ESG stands for "Environmental, Social, and Governance". It is a framework used to evaluate a company's performance in these three areas:

- Environmental: This refers to a company's impact on the environment – including factors like pollution, climate change, waste and resource conservation.

- Social: This considers a company's impact on society – including adhering to work and manufacturing practices, human rights and community involvement.

- Governance: This evaluates a company's corporate governance practices – including board structure, compliance, transparency and risk management.

Quantum computers, with their unprecedented computational power, have the potential to impact ESG practices in both positive and negative ways. These consequences will need to be considered as quantum computing develops and companies adopt quantum computing.

For example, the ability of quantum computers to process vast amounts of data and solve complex optimisation problems could enable more accurate and efficient risk assessments, supply chain tracking and resource allocation. Quantum computing could also contribute to the development of sustainable materials and renewable energy sources. Those benefits are yet unrealised but are potentially significant.

However, there are concerns regarding quantum computers that also impact ESG. Taking just some examples:

- The development and use of quantum computing raise ethical questions about data privacy and surveillance.

- There is also a potential environmental impact – the energy consumption required to power quantum computers could be significant, potentially offsetting the environmental benefits of their applications. There are currently no policies regarding energy consumption and quantum computing.[58]

- The development and control of quantum computing could be concentrated in a few powerful nations or corporations, exacerbating existing inequalities.

There is little industry guidance at present on the adoption and use of quantum computing. Examples are cited above which impact on ESG considerations, for example information published by the ICO and NQCC. In 2022, the World Economic Forum has published its first

58 World Economic Forum, "State of Quantum Computing: Building a Quantum Economy" Insight Report 2022.

Quantum Computing Governance Principles.[59] It is a useful document from a governance perspective in highlighting key themes relating to the adoption and use of quantum computing. The issues that are explored include cyber security, privacy and sustainability. Therefore, companies should consider in adopting quantum computing the impact on their broader ESG obligations.

Summary

Quantum computing has the potential to greatly assist commercial parties, as briefly explored in the section above on the practical application of quantum computing. It will therefore be an area in the future where commercial parties will need to consider the risks and benefits.

As noted in the introduction to this section, in practice a variety of issues will arise in respect of quantum computing which are of broad application to any commercial party. The fact that either one or both of the parties are adopting or using quantum computing will be irrelevant to the issue that it is being advised on.

However, there are a number of issues that will be of particular concern to either or both parties in the adoption or use of quantum computing. As explored above, the issues raised in national security and sanctions section will be relevant to acquiring assets relating to quantum computing, the section on security breaches and data protection will also be relevant to companies in discharging their data protection obligations and also confidentiality obligations. Contracting for quantum computing services will pose some unique

---

59 World Economic Forum, 'Quantum Computing Governance Principles' Insight Report 2022 available at https://www3.weforum.org/docs/WEF_Quantum_Computing_2022.pdf.

challenges in considering how an agreement will best address the concerns of both parties. The section above addressing contracting for quantum computing is a starting point for considering some of the fact specific questions that may arise in practice. Finally, we have used ESG considerations as an example of an area of law which has received more attention in recent years but will need to be considered alongside the adoption and use of quantum computing.

CHAPTER SEVEN

QUANTUM COMPUTERS AND INTELLECTUAL PROPERTY

Introduction

As set out in detail in the preceding section, quantum computing represents a paradigm shift in computer science, using the principles of quantum mechanics to perform calculations that are beyond the capabilities of classical computers. The current UK intellectual property ("**IP**") regime was not designed with quantum computers in mind, yet, as discussed below, it does offer many different forms of protection which can be applied to the different components of quantum computers. Those developing quantum technologies should consider carefully the different IP rights that may be available to them and decide how they might, in combination with contractual restrictions, trade secrets, and technological protections, protect their works and innovations.

This section is not intended to be an exhaustive recital of UK IP law, nor does it compare in any detail the rights available across different jurisdictions. It is intended to outline the IP rights available in the UK and how they might protect different aspects of quantum computers. The following IP rights and topics are addressed:

- Quantum Computing and Patents: the use of patents to protect inventions and technical processes such as quantum computing hardware, quantum algorithms, error correction methods and quantum communication techniques.

- Quantum Computing and Copyright: copyright may subsist in the code underlying quantum technologies.

- Quantum Computing and Trade Secrets: an alternative strategy for those looking to protect their quantum technologies is to rely on the law of trade secrets, which offers potentially indefinite protection if the information is not disclosed and cannot be reverse-engineered.

- IP Rights in Quantum Computer Generated Output: discussion of which IP rights may protect works or inventions generated by a quantum AI.

- A detailed case study of *Cambridge Quantum Computing Limited v 1) River Lane Research Limited 2) Dr Stephen Brierley.*[60] This case, which concerned allegations of breach of contract and misuse of confidential information, is a rarity in that it is litigation involving quantum computing. Rebecca Keating, co-author of this book, was instructed as junior counsel for the Defendants.

Quantum Computing and Patents

Introduction

The patent system in the UK is designed to incentivise innovation. A patent gives an inventor a time-limited (usually 20 year) monopoly right to prevent others from making, using, or selling an invention. Patent eligibility in the UK is governed by the Patents Act 1977. A

[60] Claim number HP-2019-000033.

patent may be granted only for an invention which is new, involves an "inventive step", and is capable of industrial application.[61]

A non-exhaustive list of things is excluded from protection, these include discoveries, literary, dramatic, musical or artistic works, computer programs, and the presentation of information. The "mathematical method" and computer program exclusions are discussed in more detail below in relation to obtaining patent protection for quantum algorithms.

The Patents Act also provides a closed list of persons to whom a patent may be granted. These persons include the inventor (or joint inventors), their employer (in specific circumstances), or the inventor's successor in title.[62]

Those seeking to patent an aspect of quantum technology should be aware of variations in international patent laws. Different jurisdictions may have varying requirements for patenting software, hardware, or algorithms.

Patent Protection for Components of Quantum Computers

A number of unique challenges are posed by the prospect of patenting quantum computing innovations. Patent examiners and eventually the courts in the UK will, in the coming years, have some complex questions to answer in relation to whether quantum computing inventions are patentable.

---

[61] Patents Act 1977, section 1(1).

[62] Patents Act 1977, s7(2).

To be considered "new", an invention must not form part of the state of the art.[63] The state of the art includes all matter which has, at any time before the priority date of the invention, been made available to the public. The invention must also involve an "inventive step"; it must not be obvious to someone skilled in the art[64], meaning it should represent a significant advancement in quantum technology. Finally, the invention must be capable of industrial application.

Given that quantum computing technologies are relatively new, and much of the research is theoretical and concerns quantum mechanics, determining novelty and non-obviousness may not be entirely straightforward. Patent examiners will need to gain the specialised knowledge to assess whether a quantum invention is, in fact, innovative.

Further, there is a "sufficiency" requirement; a patent specification must disclose the invention clearly enough and completely enough for it to be performed by a person skilled in the art.[65] In practice, an applicant should describe how the invention can be performed on physical qubits. It may be that an invention is theoretical, and does not meet the sufficiency requirement because no physical quantum computer yet exists which could implement the invention.

Various components of quantum computers are potentially eligible for patent protection, if they can fulfil the above criteria. Mauritz Kop,

---

63 Patents Act 1977, ss2(2) and 2(3).

64 Patents Act 1977, s3.

65 Patents Act 1977, s14(3).

writing in the Berkeley Technology Law Journal in 2021[66], gave as examples the technology building blocks (qubits), quantum gates and multipliers, quantum integrated circuit chips, the various types of quantum processors such as spin qubits and superconducting transmon qubits, quantum interference devices, compiler engines (i.e., optimizers, translators, mappers), decoders, the simulator and the emulator, the circuit drawer, the microarchitecture (QEX block and QEC block), the quantum-classical interface, the quantum instruction set architecture, and quantum memory.

Patentability of Quantum Algorithms

A quantum algorithm is an algorithm that runs on a quantum computer and which is typically more efficient than an algorithm run on a classical computer. While quantum computing hardware can be protected by patents, the same is not necessarily true of quantum computing software, including quantum algorithms.

In order to be granted a patent over software by the UK Intellectual Property Office, it must first be established that the software in question fulfils the requirement of s1(1) Patents Act 1977 in that it actually constitutes an "invention".

As described above, the UK, like many jurisdictions, excludes from patent protection mathematical methods and computer programs. S1(2) of the Patents Act 1977 provides (emphasis added):

66 'Quantum Computing and Intellectual Property Law', available at https://papers.ssrn.com/sol3/papers.cfm?abstract_id=3860456.

> *"it is hereby declared that the following (among other things) are not inventions for the purposes of this Act, that is to say, anything which consists of–*
>
> *(a) a discovery, scientific theory or mathematical method…*
>
> *(c) a scheme, rule, or method for performing a mental act, playing a game or doing business, or a program for a computer;*
>
> *…but the foregoing provision shall prevent anything from being treated as an invention for the purposes of this Act only to the extent that a patent or application for a patent relates to that thing as such".*

This exclusion therefore operates only if the subject matter of the patent application is a mathematical method or computer program "as such". If the invention makes a "technical contribution" to the art, it can be patented. A large amount of case law has developed around the question of how to determine what is patentable and what is a computer program "as such". At the time of writing, there is no case law in the UK governing the patentability of quantum algorithms. It is suggested, however, that the courts are likely to apply the same tests that are applied to computer programs, including AI programs.

The UK IPO's "*Manual of Patent Practice*" explains that the case of *Aerotel Ltd v Telco Holdings Ltd* [2007] RPC 7 "*provides a framework for the examiner to assess, and decide upon, the issue of excluded matter…*" The test comprises four steps, which are as follows:

- Properly construe the claim;
- Identify the actual contribution;

- Ask whether it falls solely within the excluded subject matter; and
- Check whether the actual or alleged contribution is actually technical in nature.

Kitchen LJ noted in *HTC v Apple* [2013] EWCA Civ 451 that the *Aerotel* test is followed in order to address whether the invention makes a technical contribution to the art, with the rider that novel or inventive purely excluded matter does not count as a "technical contribution".

In *AT&T Knowledge Ventures LP v Comptroller General of Patents, Designs and Trade Marks* [2009] EWHC 343 (Pat), Lewison J set out the following non-exhaustive "signposts" for consideration during the assessment of whether a computer makes a technical contribution:

> "*i) Whether the claimed technical effect has a technical effect on a process which is carried on outside the computer.*
>
> *ii) Whether the claimed technical effect operates at the level of the architecture of the computer; that is to say whether the effect is produced irrespective of the data being processed or the applications being run.*
>
> *iii) Whether the claimed technical effect results in the computer being made to operate in a new way.*
>
> *iv) Whether the program makes the computer a better computer in the sense of running more efficiently and effectively as a computer.*
>
> *v) Whether the perceived problem is overcome by the claimed invention as opposed to merely being circumvented.*"

These "signposts" have been applied by the UK IPO in the context of a patent application for a method of determining at least one unknown energy level of a physical system utilising a quantum computer (see decision O/130/22). The Hearing Officer concluded that the signposts were "*valid for quantum computer as for classical computers and still provide useful signposts as to whether the claimed invention makes a technical contribution.*"

The IP firm Marks & Clerk recommends that those considering patent protection should give thought to what technical contribution the quantum algorithm may make, and to emphasise this contribution when drafting the patent specification. It can be persuasive to explain within the specification how the *Aerotel* signposts are made out.[67]

Recent Trends in Quantum Computing Patents

A "Quantum Computing Insight Report" published by the European Patent Office ("**EPO**") in January 2023 summarised the results of patent analyses in the field of quantum computing.[68] The report identified that the number of inventions in the field of quantum computing had a grown at a rate far higher than all fields of technology in general. The above average share of international patent applications suggested high economic expectations with regard to the technologies in question and multinational commercialisation strategy.

The most important jurisdictions for patent applications for quantum technologies were the US, Japan, Europe, and China, whilst the most

---

67 https://www.marks-clerk.com/insights/articles/what-is-the-patentability-of-quantum-algorithms/#:~:text=Anything%20that%20extends%20the%20quantum,other%2C%20cutting%2Dedge%20algorithms.

68 See https://link.epo.org/web/epo_patent_insight_report-quantum_computing_en.pdf.

active applicants list was led by IBM, followed by Toshiba/Nuflare Technology, Intel, and Microsoft.

In the UK, several companies have secured patents for quantum technologies. These include Cambridge Quantum Computing, which is particularly active in the fields of quantum cryptography and quantum machine learning, Oxford Quantum Circuits, which specialises in quantum processors, and Riverlane, which develops operating systems for quantum computers.

Quantum Computing and Copyright

Copyright protection in the UK is governed by the Copyright, Designs and Patents Act 1988 (the "**CDPA**"). Copyright can subsist in original literary, dramatic, musical or artistic works, sound recordings, films, broadcasts, and typographical arrangements.[69]

Software related to quantum computing can be protected as a literary work.[70] Copyright will not, however, protect an underlying idea such as a quantum algorithm; the particular expression of the algorithm in code will be protected, but not the idea itself. Copyright does not have to be registered in the UK, it arises automatically upon creation of the work. The term of copyright protection in the UK is the life of the author plus 70 years.

In order to be protected, a work must be "original". The test for originality is whether the work is the author's own intellectual creation.[71] The originality standard is discussed further below in the

---

69 CDPA 1988, s1(1).

70 CDPA 1988, s3(1)(b).

71 See *Infopaq International v Danske Dagblades Forening* [2009] ECDR 16 (Case C-5/08).

context of quantum computer generated works. In practice, the UK courts may face challenges in distinguishing between works created by humans and those generated by quantum algorithms.

Copyright is infringed by a person who "*without the licence of the copyright owner does, or authorises another to do, any of the acts restricted by the copyright.*"[72] These acts include copying the work, issuing copies to the public, communicating the work to the public, and making an adaptation of the work.[73] Copyright infringement could become more prevalent with the increased use of quantum computers; quantum computers may be able to copy and distribute copyright works much faster than classical computers.

By contrast, quantum computers also have the capacity to bolster the enforcement of copyright law as follows:

- Quantum computers could quickly analyse vast quantities of material and identify similarities between works.
- Quantum algorithms could improve devices such as digital watermarks – invisible identifiers embedded in digital works that cannot be removed or tampered with.
- Copyright owners could use quantum blockchain technologies to manage rights and royalty payments, and quantum secure smart contracts could be used to automate transactions involving copyright works.

---

72 CDPA 1988, s16(2).

73 CDPA 1988, s16(1).

- Quantum computers will be able to monitor and record the use of copyright works more comprehensively than classical computers, leading to faster detection of unauthorised copies.

Quantum Computing and Trade Secrets

An alternative strategy for those developing, and looking to protect, quantum technologies is to rely on the law of trade secrets/confidential information. This protection is only available if the invention is not published; strict confidentiality must be maintained in the proprietary aspect of the technology. The decision whether to opt for patent protection or to keep the technology secret will involve both practical and strategic considerations. By way of example, a company may prefer to protect as trade secrets their quantum algorithms, as opposed to disclosing them in order to obtain a patent. The obvious benefits of trade secrets over patents are that trade secrets arise without registration and can be protected as for as long as they remain confidential. A trade secret which is difficult to reverse engineer could, in theory, be protected indefinitely. By contrast, patent protection lasts for just 20 years, and may be better suited to inventions which can be more easily reverse-engineered.

In the UK, trade secrets are protected by two overlapping schemes: [1] the Trade Secrets (Enforcement, etc.) Regulations 2018 (the "**Trade Secrets Regulations**") and [2] the common law. Under the Trade Secrets Regulations, trade secrets are defined as:

> "*...information which –*
>
> *(a) is secret in the sense that it is not, as a body or in the precise configuration and assembly of its components, generally known among, or readily accessible, to persons within the*

circles that normally deal with the kind of information in question,

(b) *has commercial value because it is secret, and*

(c) *has been subject to reasonable steps under the circumstances, by the person lawfully in control of the information, to keep it secret."*

It is very likely that quantum algorithms would be considered "information" and therefore would fall within the scope of the UK's trade secrets regimes.

The Trade Secrets Regulations do not that require specific measures or protections are put in place in order for information to benefit from protection as a trade secret, rather "*reasonable steps in the circumstances.*" Reasonable steps could mean marking information as confidential, access restrictions, encrypting information, or implementing contractual restrictions on disclosing the information. A record should be kept of the steps taken so that they can be proved during any litigation.

At common law, *Coco v AN Clark (Engineers) Ltd* [1968] FSR 415 sets out the test the court will apply when assessing whether there has been a breach of confidence. The information must be of a confidential nature, it must have been communicated in circumstances importing an obligation of confidence, and there must have been unauthorised use of the information to the detriment of the person communicating it.

An important practical consideration for those relying on trade secrets is maintaining secrecy when employees move on to competitors. Non-disclosure agreements and restrictive covenants will need to be agreed and robustly enforced in order to mitigate the risk of disclosures.

IP Rights in Quantum Computer Generated Output

It is no longer the case that the ability to invent, or to create literary, artistic or dramatic works, is solely a human characteristic. AI systems are now capable of devising inventions and works that, if created by a human, would be protected by IP rights. As discussed above, a likely use of quantum computers will be to power AI, resulting in improvements in the speed, accuracy, and efficiency of AI systems. A challenge for lawyers is to consider where quantum AI generated works and inventions may fit into the current intellectual property regime.

The UK Supreme Court has already decided that the requirement to identify a human inventor for the purpose of patentability means that AI-created inventions cannot be protected by a patent. It is highly unlikely that a different conclusion would be reached in the case of inventions devised by a quantum-AI.

In *Thaler v Comptroller-General of Patents, Designs and Trade Marks* [2023] UKSC 49, the Supreme Court dismissed Dr Stephen Thaler's appeal and upheld the earlier decisions that inventions where there was no named human inventor were ineligible for patent protection. Dr Thaler had asserted that two inventions were made solely by "DABUS", an autonomous AI system, and named DABUS as the inventor in patent applications. Whilst DABUS had initially been programmed and trained by a human, it had later developed so that it could, unprompted by a human, create inventions including the food container and an emergency light that were the subject of the patent applications. Neither application designated a human inventor. Dr Thaler claimed to have acquired the right to the grant of the patents by virtue of his position as owner of DABUS. The Supreme Court unanimously agreed that the word "inventor" as used in ss 7 and 13 of the Patents Act 1977, meant a natural person, and could not include a machine. Dr Thaler, the owner of the machine, had no independent right to obtain a patent in respect of any technical advance created by the machine. This judgment reached the same conclusion as in most jurisdictions where Dr Thaler had made patent applications. The Supreme Court made clear that it was not concerned with the general issue of whether inventions generated by AI systems should be patentable, rather it was answering a question which turned on the interpretation of provisions of the Patents Act 1977.

AI is already capable of creating literary, dramatic, musical and artistic works that, if created by a human, would qualify for copyright protection. Copyright law in the UK can protect computer-generated works, with the author being taken to be the person "*by whom the arrangements necessary for the creation of the works are undertaken.*"[74] It is not, however, clear how the requirement that a work be original (the author's own intellectual creation), can apply to works that have no human author.[75]

There is a tension between incentivising the use of quantum AI to foster innovation, and the traditional view that intellectual property rights reward human effort and creativity. Some legal commentators have suggested that the output created or invented by quantum or AI systems without human intervention should be in the public domain as it lacks human creativity and inventiveness, and therefore society as a whole should benefit by being able to use it.[76]

---

74 CDPA 1988, s9(3).

75 For a detailed discussion of different arguments, see The Law of Artificial Intelligence, Sweet & Maxwell, Second Edition, at §10-18.

76 "Intellectual property in quantum computing and market power: a theoretical discussion and empirical analysis" Mauritz Kop, Mateo Aboy and Timo Minssen (*Journal of Intellectual Property Law & Practice*, Volume 17, Issue 8, August 2022, pages 613–628).

Case Law on Quantum Computing: Cambridge Quantum Computing Limited v 1) River Lane Research Limited 2) Dr Stephen Brierley

Unsurprisingly given that quantum computers are not yet commonplace, there have been very few legal cases in the UK which have involved quantum computers. One case which did highlight the legal issues that can arise from the development of quantum computing was *Cambridge Quantum Computing Limited v 1) River Lane Research Limited 2) Dr Stephen Brierley* HP-2019-000033.

This Chancery Division case concerned documents created by a company engaged to provide consultancy services related to software for quantum computing. The proceedings involved allegations of breach of contract and misuse of confidential information.

The Claimant was a company which built tools for the commercialisation of quantum computers including operating systems and quantum algorithms. In July 2016, the Claimant entered into an agreement (the "**Advisory Agreement**") with the First Defendant, a company which provided consultancy services relating to the development of mathematical methods and software for quantum computing. The Second Defendant was a director of the First Defendant company and had undertaken to the Claimant to comply with various terms of the Advisory Agreement.

Pursuant to the Advisory Agreement, the First Defendant was to evaluate quantum computing research and advise the Claimant on the development of its intellectual property. A clause in the Advisory Agreement provided that any intellectual property in materials generated by the Defendants during the term of the contract would be owned by the Claimant. The Advisory Agreement also prevented the First Defendant from engaging in any activity which related to a business similar to, or competitive with, the business of the Claimant without the Claimant's consent.

In March 2017, the Claimant began to collaborate with a third party to develop an application for quantum computing. The Defendants worked on this collaboration pursuant to the terms of the Advisory Agreement.

In April 2018, the Second Defendant wrote to the Claimant giving notice of the First Defendant's termination of the Advisory Agreement with effect from 22 May 2018.

Between February 2018 and January 2019, the Defendants had published various papers and filed patent applications. The Claimant alleged that, under the terms of the Advisory Agreement, each of these papers/applications was intellectual property generated by the Defendants but owned by the Claimant. The Claimant also alleged that several of these papers/applications comprised the Claimant's confidential information. The Claimant asserted that the Defendants had breached various clauses of the Advisory Agreement and had misused the Claimant's confidential information.

In August 2019 the Claimant issued proceedings against the Defendants. It sought an injunction to prevent the Defendants from misusing or disclosing the Claimant's confidential information, damages arising from breach of contract, an inquiry into damages/account of profits, orders for disclosure/delivery up of documents relating to the business of the Claimant, a declaration that the Claimant was the owner of various patent applications, and an order requiring the Defendants to assign these applications to the Claimant. The trial was to be split with liability being dealt with first, then quantum.

In their Defence, the Defendants argued that the topic which was the subject of the collaboration between the Claimant, Defendants and third party was well known in the field of quantum computing. The technique addressed in the relevant documents (the VQE, Variational Quantum Eigensolver) had been researched by the Second Defendant prior to the signing of the Advisory Agreement. While the documents relied on by the Defendants had been created after the date of the Advisory Agreement, and were not brought to the attention of the Claimant, this was because the Defendants believed that there was no obligation to bring the same to the Claimant's attention (the "**Defendants' Documents**").

There had, the Defendants argued, been at all material times a common assumption between the parties that the Defendants would be entitled to carry out their own research and development in the area of quantum computing, (save for the relevant restrictions in the Advisory Agreement) and the Claimant's CEO had known about, and indeed encouraged, the Defendants' other quantum computing research. It was never the intention of the parties that the sole occupation of either Defendant would be to provide services to the Claimant. The Defendants argued that, in light of this common assumption, the Claimant was estopped from relying on some of the terms of the Advisory Agreement.

The Defendants also argued, as an alternative case, that a clause of the Advisory Agreement was an unenforceable restraint of trade, as the clause would have, on the Claimant's construction, prevented the Defendants carrying out their normal academic or business activities.

The Defendants challenged the subsistence and/or ownership by the Claimant of any intellectual property rights in the documents relied on by the Claimant. In addition, the Defendants argued that the content of the Defendant's Documents did not constitute a "Work" or "Invention" as defined in the Advisory Agreement. These documents, it was argued, were not created by the Defendants in the course of the provision of services under the Advisory Agreement, in particular, they did not relate to the areas of research that had been directed by the Claimant's CTO.

In respect of the allegations of misuse of confidential information, the Defendants denied that they owed the Claimant duties to keep confidential any of the material in the Defendants' Documents. They further denied that the information contained in these documents could be protected by a valid patent, or constitute protectable confidential information, as the information was either known in the art, common general knowledge, or obvious.

The claim progressed to a Case Management Conference and was listed for trial. However, the parties settled the claim on confidential terms.

This case should act as a warning for those developing quantum computing software and/or hardware, and in particular those entering into consultancy agreements in the course of that development. Lawyers tasked with drafting such agreements should be careful that the scope of the services to be provided is properly defined. Further, special care should be taken to ensure that the clauses dealing with ownership of IP rights in material generated during the agreement, as well as those establishing duties of confidence, reflect the wishes of the parties.

Summary

Whilst not designed with the quantum computing era in mind, the IP regime in the UK is most likely flexible enough to protect quantum technologies. Some possible challenges that lawyers will have to grapple with over the next few decades include advising on the best form of IP protection for the different aspects of quantum computers, be it hardware, software, or underlying data. Patent examiners will need to become familiar with the underlying technology in order to assess novelty and inventive step. Given the highly competitive nature of the quantum computing industry, it is likely that many lawyers will find themselves devising stringent confidentiality agreements to protect the most sensitive and valuable trade secrets. The boundaries of UK copyright law will be tested by quantum computers' abilities to generate rapidly new types of content. No doubt in the coming decades the courts will see cases involving IP infringement facilitated by quantum computing.

CHAPTER EIGHT

LITIGATING DISPUTES REGARDING QUANTUM COMPUTING

The widespread use of quantum computers may seem some time off. However, as described above, there have already been disputes regarding quantum computers. Therefore, it is worth considering how practically parties can deal with issues that may arise in disputes regarding quantum computers.

Take, for example, the issue of appointing an expert. In any technical dispute appointing the appropriate expert is an important element in the ultimate success of a case. While this is not a unique concern in the context of technical disputes, disputes regarding quantum computers pose unique challenges.

The first is the difficulty in appointing an independent expert in the required field. Quantum computers itself is a blunt reference to a variety of different specialisms. Locating an appropriately qualified expert poses its own challenges, as does locating an expert who is independent to the parties involved. This is before one considers other issues which are always important in appointing an expert such as their experience of being an expert witness, availability, cost and if the expert is willing to be involved at all.

Therefore, while it is always important to consider the need for expert opinion early on in a technical dispute, this will be particularly important in the context of disputes regarding quantum computers.

Secondly, and connected with the first point, while not an approach favoured in many disputes (largely due to cost) it is worth considering whether it may be appropriate to appoint multiple experts. For example, if a dispute required expert input from an individual with experience of designing quantum algorithms for use in proposing new drugs for a pharmaceutical company, it may be necessary to get two experts [1] an expert in designing algorithms for quantum computers more generally and [2] an expert in the specific drug or in the pharmaceutical industry.

CHAPTER NINE

APPROACH IN OTHER JURISDICTIONS

Although this book is focussed on quantum computing in the UK, and the law of England and Wales, the rapid growth of quantum computing around the world and the different approaches to regulation are briefly summarised in this section.

The USA

The USA is a global leader in quantum computing research. The National Quantum Initiative Act was passed in December 2018 and authorises various government agencies to fund activities promoting quantum science. Funding is allocated to laboratories, universities and private companies. Like the UK, the USA imposes strict controls on the export of quantum technology through, *inter alia,* the International Traffic in Arms Regulations and Export Administration Regulations.

The EU

In 2018 the EU launched the Quantum Flagship Program, a 10-year scheme which promised 1 billion of investment into the development of quantum technologies including quantum computers and quantum communication. Export controls in the EU are governed in part by EU-wide regulations, and in part by national laws. As discussed above in Chapter Four, the Dual-Use regulation applies to technologies with military or cryptographic applications.

China

The Chinese government has made substantial investment in quantum computing, and has established a National Laboratory for Quantum Information Sciences. China tightly restricts the export of advanced technologies including quantum computers.

International Agreements

Some international regimes have been established to promote regional and international security and stability. The Wassenaar Arrangement on Export Controls for Conventional Arms and Dual-Use Goods and Technologies, of which the UK is one of 42 members, is an agreement that was first established in 1996 and which sets voluntary export control policies for conventional weapons and "dual-use" goods (those which have both civilian and military applications). The list of goods which are subject to the Wassenaar Agreement is updated annually to reflect emerging technologies, and recent updates have focused on quantum computing components and technologies.

FUTURE DEVELOPMENTS AND CONCLUSION

Predictions vary as to when quantum computers will achieve quantum advantage. In the coming years, there will not only be significant developments in quantum computing technology but also increased regulation, industry comments and case law. The exact shape of this is not yet known. The future is exciting and as always, uncertain.

MORE BOOKS BY LAW BRIEF PUBLISHING

A selection of our other titles available now:-

'A Practical Guide to Probation Breaches and Other Applications' by Mark Thomas
'A Practical Guide to Remarriage and Divorce' by Cordelia Williams & Claire Howard
'A Practical Guide to Privacy, Transparency, Reporting Restrictions and Closed Proceedings in the Court of Protection' by Laura Mannering
'Beaumont on Barristers – A Guide to Defending Disciplinary Proceedings (Second Edition)' by Marc Beaumont
'A Practical Guide to Payments for Environmental Services' by Ben Sharples
'A Practical Guide to the Law of Pregnancy and Maternity at Work' by Rebecca Thomas
'A Practical Guide to Redundancy – Second Edition' by Philip Hyland & Collette Moore
'A Practical Guide to International Issues for Scottish Family Lawyers' by Susie Mountain, Donna McKay, Ken MacDonald
'A Practical Guide to the Law on Deprivation of Liberty' by Ben Troke
'A Practical Guide to Rights over Airspace and Subsoil – Second Edition' by Daniel Gatty
'A Practical Guide to the Law in Relation to Inquests' by Ramya Nagesh
'A Practical Guide to the Construction and Rectification of Wills and Trust Instruments (Second Edition)' by Edward Hewitt
'A Practical Guide to Data Protection in Social Housing' by Clare Paterson
'A Practical Guide to Spousal Maintenance – Second Edition' by Liz Cowell
'A Practical Guide to International Parental Child Abduction Law (England and Wales)' by Dr Onyója Momoh
'A Practical Guide to Deprivation of British Citizenship' by Sean Ell
'A Practical Guide to Commercial Property Service Charges' by Rachel Garton
'A Practical Guide to Clinical Negligence – Third Edition' by Geoffrey Simpson-Scott (Geoff)
'A Practical Guide to the Rights of Grandparents in Children Proceedings – Second Edition' by Stuart Barlow

'The Electronic Communications Code: A Practical Guide – Second Edition' by Kerry Bretherton KC, James Castle, Mark Loveday

'A Practical Guide to the Independent School Standards – September 2023 Edition' by Sarah McKimm

'A Practical Guide to Estate Administration and Crypto Assets' by Richard Marshall

'A Practical Guide to Parental Alienation in Private and Public Law Children Cases' by Sam King QC & Frankie Shama

'Contested Heritage – Removing Art from Land and Historic Buildings' by Richard Harwood QC, Catherine Dobson, David Sawtell

'The Limits of Separate Legal Personality: When Those Running a Company Can Be Held Personally Liable for Losses Caused to Third Parties Outside of the Company' by Dr Mike Wilkinson

'A Practical Guide to Transgender Law' by Robin Moira White & Nicola Newbegin

'A Practical Guide to 'Stranded Spouses' in Family Law' by Mani Singh Basi

'A Practical Guide to Residential Freehold Conveyancing' by Lorraine Richardson

'A Practical Guide to Pensions on Divorce for Lawyers' by Bryan Scant

'A Practical Guide to Challenging Sham Marriage Allegations in Immigration Law' by Priya Solanki

'A Practical Guide to Digital Communications Evidence in Criminal Law' by Sam Willis

'A Practical Guide to Legal Rights in Scotland' by Sarah-Jane Macdonald

'A Practical Guide to New Build Conveyancing' by Paul Sams & Rebecca East

'A Practical Guide to Inherited Wealth on Divorce' by Hayley Trim

'A Practical Guide to Practice Direction 12J and Domestic Abuse in Private Law Children Proceedings' by Rebecca Cross & Malvika Jaganmohan

'A Practical Guide to Confiscation and Restraint' by Narita Bahra QC, John Carl Townsend, David Winch

'A Practical Guide to the Law of Forests in Scotland' by Philip Buchan

'A Practical Guide to Health and Medical Cases in Immigration Law' by Rebecca Chapman & Miranda Butler

'A Practical Guide to Bad Character Evidence for Criminal Practitioners by Aparna Rao

'A Practical Guide to Extradition Law post-Brexit' by Myles Grandison et al

'A Practical Guide to Hoarding and Mental Health for Housing Lawyers' by Rachel Coyle

'Stephens on Contractual Indemnities' by Richard Stephens
'A Practical Guide to the EU Succession Regulation' by Richard Frimston
'A Practical Guide to Solicitor and Client Costs – Second Edition' by Robin Dunne
'Constructive Dismissal – Practice Pointers and Principles' by Benjimin Burgher
'A Practical Guide to Religion and Belief Discrimination Claims in the Workplace' by Kashif Ali
'A Practical Guide to the Law of Medical Treatment Decisions' by Ben Troke
'Fundamental Dishonesty and QOCS in Personal Injury Proceedings: Law and Practice' by Jake Rowley
'A Practical Guide to the Law in Relation to School Exclusions' by Charlotte Hadfield & Alice de Coverley
'A Practical Guide to Divorce for the Silver Separators' by Karin Walker
'The Right to be Forgotten – The Law and Practical Issues' by Melissa Stock
'A Practical Guide to Planning Law and Rights of Way in National Parks, the Broads and AONBs' by James Maurici QC, James Neill et al
'A Practical Guide to Election Law' by Tom Tabori
'A Practical Guide to the Law in Relation to Surrogacy' by Andrew Powell
'A Practical Guide to Claims Arising from Fatal Accidents – Second Edition' by James Patience
'A Practical Guide to Asbestos Claims' by Jonathan Owen & Gareth McAloon
'A Practical Guide to Stamp Duty Land Tax in England and Northern Ireland' by Suzanne O'Hara
'A Practical Guide to the Law of Farming Partnerships' by Philip Whitcomb
'A Practical Guide to the Law of Unlawful Eviction and Harassment – Second Edition' by Stephanie Lovegrove
'A Practical Guide to Costs in Personal Injury Claims – Second Edition' by Matthew Hoe
'A Practical Guide to the General Data Protection Regulation (GDPR) – Second Edition' by Keith Markham
'A Practical Guide to Working with Litigants in Person and McKenzie Friends in Family Cases' by Stuart Barlow
'Protecting Unregistered Brands: A Practical Guide to the Law of Passing Off' by Lorna Brazell
'A Practical Guide to Secondary Liability and Joint Enterprise Post-Jogee' by Joanne Cecil & James Mehigan

'A Practical Guide to the Pre-Action RTA Claims Protocol for Personal Injury Lawyers' by Antonia Ford

'A Practical Guide to Neighbour Disputes and the Law' by Alexander Walsh

'A Practical Guide to Coercive Control for Legal Practitioners and Victims' by Rachel Horman

'A Practical Guide to the Law of Driverless Cars – Second Edition'

by Alex Glassbrook, Emma Northey & Scarlett Milligan

'A Practical Guide to TOLATA Claims' by Greg Williams

'A Practical Guide to Elderly Law – Second Edition' by Justin Patten

'A Practical Guide to Responding to Housing Disrepair and Unfitness Claims' by Iain Wightwick

'A Practical Guide to the Law of Bullying and Harassment in the Workplace' by Philip Hyland

'How to Be a Freelance Solicitor: A Practical Guide to the SRA-Regulated Freelance Solicitor Model' by Paul Bennett

'A Practical Guide to Prison Injury Claims' by Malcolm Johnson

'A Practical Guide to Advising Clients at the Police Station' by Colin Stephen McKeown-Beaumont

'A Practical Guide to Antisocial Behaviour Injunctions – Second Edition' by Iain Wightwick

'Practical Mediation: A Guide for Mediators, Advocates, Advisers, Lawyers, and Students in Civil, Commercial, Business, Property, Workplace, and Employment Cases' by Jonathan Dingle with John Sephton

'The Mini-Pupillage Workbook' by David Boyle

'A Practical Guide to Crofting Law' by Brian Inkster

'A Practical Guide to the Law of Domain Names and Cybersquatting' by Andrew Clemson

'A Practical Guide to the Law of Gender Pay Gap Reporting' by Harini Iyengar

'NHS Whistleblowing and the Law' by Joseph England

'Employment Law and the Gig Economy' by Nigel Mackay & Annie Powell

'A Practical Guide to Noise Induced Hearing Loss (NIHL) Claims' by Andrew Mckie, Ian Skeate, Gareth McAloon

'An Introduction to Beauty Negligence Claims – A Practical Guide for the Personal Injury Practitioner' by Greg Almond

'Intercompany Agreements for Transfer Pricing Compliance' by Paul Sutton

'Zen and the Art of Mediation' by Martin Plowman

'A Practical Guide to Adoption for Family Lawyers' by Graham Pegg

'A Practical Guide to Industrial Disease Claims' by Andrew Mckie & Ian Skeate
'A Practical Guide to Conducting a Sheriff Court Proof' by Andrew Stevenson
'A Practical Guide to Vicarious Liability' by Mariel Irvine
'A Practical Guide to Applications for Landlord's Consent and Variation of Leases' by Mark Shelton
'A Practical Guide to Relief from Sanctions Post-Mitchell and Denton' by Peter Causton
'A Practical Guide to Equity Release for Advisors' by Paul Sams
'A Practical Guide to Financial Services Claims' by Chris Hegarty
'A Practical Guide to Financial Ombudsman Service Claims' by Adam Temple & Robert Scrivenor
'A Practical Guide to Running Housing Disrepair and Cavity Wall Claims – Second Edition' by Andrew Mckie & Ian Skeate
'A Practical Guide to Holiday Sickness Claims – Second Edition' by Andrew Mckie & Ian Skeate
'Arguments and Tactics for Personal Injury and Clinical Negligence Claims' by Dorian Williams
'A Practical Guide to Drone Law' by Rufus Ballaster, Andrew Firman, Eleanor Clot
'On Experts: CPR35 for Lawyers and Experts' by David Boyle
'An Introduction to Personal Injury Law' by David Boyle

These books and more are available to order online direct from the publisher at www.lawbriefpublishing.com, where you can also read free sample chapters. For any queries, call us on 0844 587 2383 or email us at mail@lawbriefpublishing.com.

Our books are all generally in stock at www.amazon.co.uk with free next day delivery for Prime members, and at good legal bookshops such as Wildy & Sons.

We are regularly launching new books in our series of practical day-to-day practitioners' guides. Visit our website and join our free newsletter to be kept informed and to receive special offers, free chapters, etc.

You can also follow us on Twitter at www.twitter.com/lawbriefpub.

www.ingramcontent.com/pod-product-compliance
Lightning Source LLC
LaVergne TN
LVHW022112200926
848481LV00003B/1142
9781916698604